MW01089634

SOMETHING *Sweet*

Desserts, Baked Goods, and Treats for Every Occasion

Recipes and photos by
Miriam Pascal
creator of
OvertimeCook.com

Published by **ARTSCROLL / SHAAR PRESS**
4401 Second Avenue / Brooklyn, NY 11232 / (718) 921-9000
www.artscroll.com

Distributed in Israel by **SIFRIATI / A. GITLER**
Moshav Magshimim / Israel

Distributed in Europe by **LEHMANNS**
Unit E, Viking Business Park, Rolling Mill Road
Jarrow, Tyne and Wear, NE32 3DP / England

Distributed in Australia and New Zealand by **GOLDS WORLD OF JUDAICA**
3-13 William Street / Balaclava, Melbourne 3183, Victoria / Australia

Distributed in South Africa by **KOLLEL BOOKSHOP**
Northfield Centre / 17 Northfield Avenue / Glenhazel 2192
Johannesburg, South Africa

ISBN-10: 1-4226-1615-0 / ISBN-13: 978-1-4226-1615-4

Printed in Canada

Acknowledgments

THANK YOU TO ...

First and foremost, to HASHEM, for blessing me with so much and for giving me the strengths and talents to produce this book and for providing me with everything exactly when I need it.

My parents, HARRY and NECHAMA PASCAL, for supporting me and putting up with me throughout the process of writing this book, and especially for teaching me from a young age to be bold and confident in the kitchen.

My siblings, YAAKOV and FREIDI, YONI and CHAYA, EZRA and SARAH, MORDY and CHEVY, and DEVORAH, for constantly offering your help and assistance — and kitchens — for the cause.

My nieces, CHAYALA, MIRI, MIRIAM, TOVA, ALIZA, and SARA, for being the best — and most honest — taste-testers, and for inspiring me to create so many of these treats for you.

BRUCHA BILLER, for being a better friend than I'll ever deserve. And to MRS. SHMAYE, SHAINDY, and ALL OF MY SHMAYE "SISTERS," for helping me truly understand the meaning of the phrase "friends are the family we choose for ourselves."

All of my friends and blog friends who have helped me, supported me, encouraged me, and stepped in whenever help was needed. Special thanks to LIVIYA KUSHNER, YITTY KATZ, CARLA CARDELLO, and SHANNA SCHAD. And an extra special thank-you to MIRIAM ROSENTHAL for keeping me organized!

LEAH SCHAPIRA, for recognizing my potential so early on, and becoming an amazing guide, mentor, and friend.

VICTORIA DWEK, my fabulous editor at *Ami's Whisk Magazine*. And to RECHY FRANKFURTER, for welcoming me into the wonderful world of *Ami*.

NANCY RABIN, for finding and sending me Grandma's recipes, so I can share her wonderful food with the world.

My awesome baking assistants who helped create the treats on these pages: AVA ZUCKER, MELISSA KAYE, and SARI ELLER. And to the talented people whose expertise enhanced the recipes and features of this book, TZIVI JACUBOVIC, CHARLES SAYEGH, SHAINDEL SIEV, AVROHOM PERL and MOSHE STATMAN.

To party-planner CHAVI CHASE (pretapartee@gmail.com), for sharing her expertise and experience for the Party Guide.

RABBI MEIR ZLOTOWITZ, for giving me this amazing opportunity.

GEDALIAH ZLOTOWITZ, for believing in me from day one, and encouraging and guiding me — and my book — every step of the way.

MRS. FELICE EISNER, for patiently editing my writing, for the careful attention to detail that makes this book so great, and for teaching me to be a better writer.

DEVORAH BLOCH, for turning my abstract visions and vague descriptions into a beautiful masterpiece.

The proofreaders, TOVA OVITS and JUDI DICK, for working under tight deadlines to perfect my book.

Last, but certainly not least, to my loyal FANS and FOLLOWERS, who have driven me to keep going, keep innovating, and keep striving to be better. You believed in this book before I did, and I hope I've met your expectations.

Table of

Contents

Introduction

I never intended for any of this to happen.

It started a couple of years ago, when I was working at a boring corporate job. I'm a creative person and I needed an outlet for my creativity. After trying my hand at a number of hobbies, I began to experiment in the kitchen. Cooking and baking have always been activities I enjoyed, but I quickly discovered that by inventing new recipes, I had found the creative outlet I was so desperately seeking.

August 7th, 2011 is the day everything changed. I combined my newfound interest in creating recipes with my budding interest in photography and my lifelong love of writing and … *OvertimeCook.com* was born. I posted my first recipe that day: Peanut Butter Truffle Stuffed Oreos, followed by Hearty Split Pea Soup the next day. Those weren't the most sophisticated recipes, and the photos, by my current standards, weren't good at all. But I was having fun, and honestly, I figured that a week or two later, I would move on to another hobby.

Then an amazing thing happened. People started to visit my website. That August, I had 634 visits to overtimecook.com. Probably about half of them were just me, checking on my site. Another quarter of them were probably my mother, getting *nachas*. But the people I didn't even know started to visit and to comment. The next month, I had 1673 visits to my blog, and by February of 2012, my site broke the ten-thousand hit mark. I quickly developed a reputation for two things: creative and delicious kosher desserts, and approachable, family-friendly food. My blog now gets hundreds of thousands of visitors every month, and it's an honor to be able to enhance people's meals through my recipes.

And that's really what all of this is about: enhancing people's lives through food and sharing recipes. Some of my favorite comments over the years come from readers who have incorporated my recipes into their daily lives. "My husband thinks I became a better cook," said one excited reader, "but really I've been making all of your recipes!" Another reader noted, "Not a Shabbos, a holiday, a special occasion, or even a weekly menu goes by without our enjoying at least one Overtime Cook recipe."

Over the years, I've had the pleasure of interacting with tens of thousands of my fans and readers through comments, email, and live appearances. Those interactions taught me so much, and they helped me grow as a recipe developer. Through the requests of my fans, I learned what people wanted — and didn't want — in a recipe. My recipes and my entire cooking style have been shaped by this interactive experience.

But that's just half of my culinary journey. It actually started when I was a little kid.

Growing up in my mother's kitchen, I just assumed that all mothers were great cooks, and that all of them would pull together creative flavor combinations to create exciting new dishes. I took it for granted that when we enjoyed a dish in a restaurant, my mother would taste it and figure out how to make it at home.

My mother, the most creative cook I've ever met (far more creative than I am!), has instilled in me a fearlessness in the kitchen that paved the way for me to take the plunge and start creating recipes. From my father, I learned the importance of precision in cooking and baking, and why it's important to always use the correct tool for the job. I learned the difference between large dice and small dice, why everyone needs a big, sharp chef's knife, and how being fanatical about details makes you a better cook. This knowledge and experience were instrumental when I began to measure and record my recipes and they help ensure success for my readers. I was fortunate enough to grow up in a "foodie" household, even before anyone knew what a "foodie" was, and I'm extra fortunate to be able to pass on to such a large number of people the knowledge and skills that my parents instilled in me.

Whether I was developing and testing the recipes, or whether I was styling and shooting the photos, this book was designed with you, the reader, in mind. It is meant to be, above all, practical and useful. I thought of every occasion — be it a simple weekday afternoon, a beautiful dessert table at an engagement party, and everything in between — and created a treat that's perfect for that occasion. Because life is always better with **Something Sweet**.

Enjoy, and happy baking!

Miriam

overtimecook.com | overtimecook@gmail.com

PLAN AHEAD

You'll find "plan ahead" instructions on every page. These detailed instructions will help you successfully bake and prepare ahead of time for a party, holiday, or any other occasion. However, it's important to remember that no matter the recipe, fresh treats will always taste at least slightly better than frozen ones.

DAIRY OR PAREVE

Every recipe here indicates if it's dairy, pareve (nondairy), or works either way. Almost every recipe offers a pareve option, but the flavor of real dairy will generally be tastier than the nondairy option.

Baking Guide

☐ **FLOUR** Unless otherwise specified, use all-purpose flour. For recipes using whole wheat flour, my preference is for white whole wheat flour, which is made from a variety of wheat that's considered "albino" — that is, lighter in both color and flavor— but that is nutritionally the same as standard whole wheat.

☐ **COCOA POWDER** There are two types of cocoa powder: Unsweetened (Regular) Cocoa Powder and Dutch Process Cocoa Powder. They are **not** interchangeable! Dutch process is cocoa that has undergone a process to neutralize the acid. This makes for a darker, more chocolatey flavored product, but it also means that the scientific makeup of it is different. For example, in recipes using baking soda, which requires an acid to react, Dutch process cocoa (which had its acid removed) will not work. In general, unless a recipe specifies Dutch process, always use regular unsweetened cocoa powder. Some brands of cocoa are not clear about whether or not they are Dutch process (using wording such as "Imported from Holland"), which can cause you to purchase the wrong kind. Therefore, I've tested all of the recipes in this book using Hershey's cocoa powder, which is always clearly marked.

☐ **MILK OR SOY MILK** If you're baking dairy, it's likely that you keep milk in the fridge, so adding some to recipes shouldn't be a challenge. However, if most of your baking (like mine) is nondairy, you'll find yourself using soy milk all the time, which you might not have handy.

I've come up with two solutions to this minor problem. The first is to keep "juice box"-size soy milk cartons in my pantry. They last a while, and the 8-ounce size makes them perfect for cakes and the like.

I know that there are times when I'll need a small amount (such as a cookie that calls for 2 tablespoons or a glaze that calls for a few teaspoons), so I freeze soy milk in ice cube trays. Measure out one tablespoon per cavity. Once frozen, remove cubes from the tray and place in a bag until ready to use. When you need a small amount, defrost a cube or two.

☐ **EGGS** Unless otherwise specified, use large eggs in recipes.

☐ **BUTTER OR MARGARINE** Because I most often bake nondairy, I generally don't use butter. Because the substitute for it is margarine, which is considered pretty unhealthy, I try to avoid it wherever possible. In this book, I only use it in recipes where it's absolutely necessary for the texture of the finished product. When I do use margarine, I use trans-fat-free versions, which don't have the same unhealthy characteristics as the old-fashioned kind.

☐ **LEAVENING AGENTS** These are the additives that make your baked goods rise and give them the correct texture. Leaveners include baking soda, baking powder, yeast, and cream of tartar. For best results, always use the specific leavening agent called for in the recipe.

Baking Soda reacts with acid (such as brown sugar or lemon juice) in the batter or dough to produce carbon dioxide, which expands the baked goods and produces an airier result.

Baking Powder contains baking soda, as well as an acidic additive such as cream of tartar, which helps it react. Baking powder loses its potency after some time; for best results, an open container should be replaced after three months.

☐ **VANILLA** Vanilla is an ingredient that I feel very passionately about. While people often think of "vanilla flavor" as the absence of any "real" flavor, vanilla is, in fact, a really great flavor on its own. Some people believe that artificial vanilla is just as good as real vanilla, but I humbly disagree. You simply can't compare the taste!

Vanilla comes in a number of forms, the most popular of which is vanilla extract. You can also get vanilla beans, vanilla sugar, and vanilla bean paste. My personal favorite is the paste (I love the little flecks of vanilla bean that show in the final product, as well as, of course, the strong vanilla flavor), but they're all interchangeable in the following measurements:

1 vanilla bean pod = 1 teaspoon vanilla extract = 1 teaspoon vanilla bean paste = 1 Tablespoon vanilla sugar

☐ **SUGARS** There are a number of different types of sugar, and it's important to always use the correct one for each recipe.

Granulated Sugar, Sugar When a recipe calls for "sugar," I am referring to good old-fashioned granulated sugar, so use this unless otherwise specified.

Powdered Sugar Also called confectioner's sugar, this is sugar that has been ground into a very fine powder. Powdered sugar is often used for its textural properties in applications such as frostings and glazes. It's also used for decoration, and can be sprinkled or sifted over baked goods, especially dark-colored treats, for a pretty contrast.

Brown Sugar comes in two forms, dark brown sugar and light brown sugar. Dark brown sugar has a higher concentration of molasses and a deeper flavor than light brown sugar. In general, these two are interchangeable, especially if the recipe doesn't specify which to use.

☐ **CREAM CHEESE** Many of these recipes call for cream cheese; they've also all been tested with a soy-based substitute. I used the Tofutti brand. While there are some differences between soy and dairy cream cheese, soy cream cheese does work well as a nondairy substitute. (The same can be said for sour cream.)

All the recipes in this book should be made with bar (unwhipped) cream cheese. Whipped cream cheese will not produce the desired results.

CITRUS ZEST Of all baking ingredients, fresh citrus zest is the most irreplaceable. Readers often ask me if they can skip it, or replace it with something else, and the answer is ... not really. I don't enjoy zesting citrus fruits either, but the fresh flavor that comes through in the final product is not something you can get anywhere else. If you do skip it (especially in a recipe like the Triple Citrus Bundt Cake (page 66), the flavor just won't be the same.

For the easiest zesting option, consider investing in a good microplane zester. If you don't have one, use the smallest holes of a box grater.

When removing the zest from the fruit, make sure to remove just the outer, colored part. The white part (pith) is bitter, and shouldn't be included in your baked goods.

CHOCOLATE A general rule about chocolate (and really, most ingredients) is that the better quality you start with, the better the end result will be. When using it in a recipe, especially where it's the dominant flavor (such as **Salted Chocolate Peanut Butter Tartlets** (page 124), or **Chocolate Truffles** (page 158), start with the best chocolate you can find and/or afford.

The cocoa percentage of of chocolate will indicate how it will taste. Higher cocoa content means darker, richer and more bitter chocolate flavor. Chocolate purists often enjoy 72% cocoa, but if you don't like yours so bitter, try a lower percentage.

Milk and white chocolate cannot be used interchangeably with dark chocolate. When coating an item in either milk or white chocolate, use extreme caution while melting, as it is more difficult to work with than dark chocolate. Additionally, melted milk or white chocolate will be thicker than melted dark chocolate, so you may need to thin it out with a few drops of oil when using it.

INGREDIENT SUBSTITUTIONS

SWEETENED CONDENSED MILK Combine ⅓ cup boiling water, 4 Tablespoons butter or margarine, ¾ cup sugar and 1 cup milk powder in a bowl. Mix, preferably with an electric mixer, until smooth. Store in refrigerator for up to a week. This yields the equivalent of one 14-ounce can.

BUTTERMILK Place 1 Tablespoon lemon juice into a one-cup measuring cup. Fill the remainder of the cup with milk or soy milk. Set it aside for a few minutes until it curdles; use in place of buttermilk.

BOURBON While not a perfect substitute, especially for larger amounts, a small amount of bourbon in a recipe can be replaced with one part vanilla extract and two parts water. Note that when used in baking, there's no need to use "good" whiskey. I keep a bottle of inexpensive bourbon on hand, and use it just for baking.

BROWN SUGAR Combine 1 cup sugar with 1 Tablespoon molasses in a small bowl. Mix until completely combined and mixture resembles brown sugar.

☐ **MIXER ATTACHMENTS** There are three main attachments that often come with an electric mixer: the whisk, the paddle, and the dough hook.

Whisk The wires of the whisk attachment are used for beating ingredients such as cream and egg whites. Because the wires aren't as firm as other attachments, the whisk isn't ideal for heavy mixes, such as doughs.

Dough Hook The dough hook is a firm attachment used for kneading dough. The shape of this attachment isn't ideal for beating softer items, such as cake batters or egg whites, which need to be more thoroughly incorporated.

Paddle While not standard with all mixers, this is the attachment I use most in baking. Somewhere between the whisk and the dough hook, it's stiff enough to handle thick batter and dough, but it will incorporate all the ingredients well, like the whisk attachment. This is my attachment of choice for all cookie doughs and batters. If your mixer doesn't come with one, it's worthwhile to purchase it if you're a frequent baker.

Beater Often the only attachment to come with inexpensive hand mixers, this is a cross between the whisk and the paddle, and is a suitable replacement for either, but will usually not hold up well to stiff doughs, such as yeast doughs.

☐ **RUBBER SPATULA** While not the flashiest tool, a rubber spatula is a must-have for dessert making. Whether you need to scrape down the sides of the bowl to incorporate all the ingredients, flip a crepe, or incorporate whipped cream into a mousse, you'll pick this up time and again. I like to use a heavy, sturdy silicone spatula, sometimes called an omelette turner.

☐ **WET VS. DRY MEASURING CUPS** When measuring wet ingredients, use a larger measuring cup, or a **liquid measuring cup** with the amounts measured on the sides. Because liquid fall evenly, it's easy to measure the correct amount. For solids, which don't form a neat line across the cup, it's better to use **dry measuring cups**, or cups that each contain a specific amount of the ingredient. My personal favorite set has 19 pieces, including a ⅔ cup measuring cup, a ¾ cup, 1½ cups, etc. It saves a ton of time when measuring.

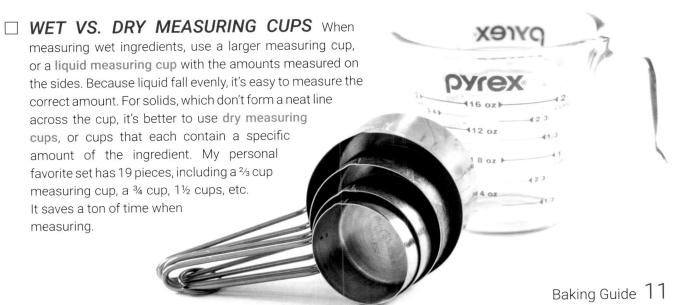

☐ *BAKING SHEETS AND OTHER PANS*

Many people I know use disposable baking pans, which make cleanup a breeze. However, baking in real pans will yield better results than the disposable sort. Specifically, I only use real (nonstick, heavy) baking sheets. Lining them with a silicone mat or parchment paper makes cleanup a snap, and the results will be more evenly baked treats.

Bundt Pans A good quality bundt pan can make all the difference between a cake that slides right out and a cake that breaks and sticks when you try to remove it. Disposable bundt pans just don't do the job as well, so I don't generally recommend them. Silicone bundt pans can cause your cake to become misshapen, and are hard to wash, so I don't like them. I use nonstick bundt pans. My method for removing bundt cakes from the pan was tested with nonstick Nordic Ware pans.

When choosing the shape, beware of overly complex shapes, which can cause difficulty in removing the cake.

☐ *SQUEEZE BOTTLES*

When decorating dessert plates (see page 126 for tips), a squeeze bottle comes in handy. Store-bought sauces often come in a squeeze bottle, but keep a couple of others on hand for homemade sauces (page 194-195), which taste so much better!

TIPS

☐ *HOW TO GLAZE A CAKE*

Always wait for your cake to cool completely. It's important for the glaze to have the correct consistency. If the glaze is too thin, it will run off the cake or dissolve right into it. Don't hesitate to use a bit more powdered sugar than the recipe calls for — you want the glaze to be the thickest possible while still being spreadable.

Once the glaze has been made, spoon it over the center of the cake carefully, and gently guide it down the sides with a spoon. Alternatively, you can tap the cake plate gently on the counter to force the glaze down the sides.

☐ *HOW TO MEASURE INGREDIENTS*

In baking, it's important to measure ingredients very carefully, especially dry ingredients. The best way to measure a dry ingredient (like flour) is to spoon it into a measuring cup, then level it off with a knife. This will ensure that the cup is full, but not overfull, and not packed too densely.

☐ *HOW TO FREEZE YOUR DESSERTS FOR BEST RESULTS*

Air kills baked goods and causes freezer burn. When frozen properly, most of the desserts in this book will last nicely. The first trick is to use heavy-duty foil. Cheap, thin foil, even when doubled or tripled, will not hold up as well.

Second, after wrapping your item in foil, place it into a large plastic bag and seal the bag. This will ensure it stays airtight throughout the freezing process.

Before wrapping and placing your treats into the freezer, allow them to fully cool. Otherwise, condensation from the cooling dessert will freeze and cause the dessert to become soggy when you defrost it.

☐ *THE BEST TEMPERATURE FOR INGREDIENTS*

Unless otherwise specified, use room temperature ingredients, such as butter, margarine, and eggs.

☐ HOW TO MEASURE STICKY SUBSTANCES

When measuring sticky substances like honey, peanut butter, or marshmallow fluff, you don't want half of it to stay behind, stuck to the cup. The simple way around this is to spray your measuring cup with nonstick cooking spray before measuring. Even simpler, if the amount of the sticky ingredient is the same as the amount of oil in the recipe, measure the oil first, then use the same cup to measure the sticky ingredient.

☐ HOW TO MELT CHOCOLATE

The best way to melt chocolate is to use the double-boiler method. While you can buy a double boiler, you definitely don't need to. Simply place a small pot of water on the stove and bring it to a boil. Next, place a small heatproof bowl (metal or glass) over it. Choose a bowl that completely covers the pot rim. Place the chocolate into the bowl and stir occasionally until it has melted.

Keep melted chocolate in the bowl, and if it hardens as you use it, place it back over the pot of boiling water and melt it again.

Use caution when melting chocolate: If it comes into contact with water, the chocolate will seize up and not melt properly.

☐ CONVERSIONS

The main thing you have to remember is that 1 cup = 16 Tablespoons and 1 Tablespoon = 3 teaspoons. Everything else can be figured out from there:

⅛ cup = 2 Tablespoons

¼ cup = 4 Tablespoons

½ cup = 8 Tablespoons

¾ cup = 12 Tablespoons

Most importantly, make sure to have fun! Baking is a fun activity — involve the children, indulge your creativity, and enjoy creating sweet treats.

☐ HOW TO REMOVE A CAKE FROM THE PAN

To remove your desserts from the pan, it's important to grease and flour the pan sufficiently. Don't skimp on the nonstick spray, then sprinkle a dusting of flour over the greased pan. Turn the pan upside down and tap it to shake off the excess flour, as that can cause the cake to stick as well. See page 52 for full instructions on removing a bundt cake from the pan.

☐ HOW TO WHIP SOFT OR STIFF PEAKS

When beating egg whites or cream, the instructions will often tell you to beat to soft peaks or stiff peaks. What's the difference? Soft peaks are just starting to hold their shape, but are loose and fall back into themselves after a few seconds. Stiff peaks, on the other hand, are firm and will continue to hold their shape. It's important to ensure that the whites are beaten to the correct texture, or the end result will not have the right texture.

However, be sure not to over-beat the cream or egg whites, as that will affect the end result as well.

☐ HOW TO ENSURE SUCCESS IN ALL RECIPES

Be sure to read through the entire recipe before you start. Make sure you understand everything, that you have everything, and that you're aware of any time lapses that need to occur during the process.

All the recipes in this book were tested — and enjoyed — by at least two people other than myself. In order to make sure you achieve success, it's important to stick to the recipe exactly. Some substitutes are commonly used, and feel free to experiment, but bear in mind that baking is a science, and any changes can have an adverse affect on the final product.

■ One of the most important kitchen tools you can use is a cookie scoop. Not only does it ensure that your cookies all look uniform, but it also ensures that they are all the same size, which leads to even baking. If you buy only one, medium is the size to get. I like to use a small cookie scoop as well, for occasions when I want a smaller cookie, such as when making sandwich cookies. In place of a level cookie scoop worth of dough, use a heaping tablespoon for medium and a heaping teaspoon for small.

■ Why use a cooling rack? They allow air to circulate around the bottoms of the cookies, preventing condensation that can lead to slightly soggy cookies.

■ Bottoms of your cookies too dark? A number of things can cause this problem. First, place your oven rack higher, as the bottom third of some ovens is more prone to cause burning. Second, use light colored cookie sheets, as dark ones have more of a tendency to burn.

COOKIES
AND BARS

■ For fresh-out-of-the-oven cookies when time is limited, scoop cookie dough into balls and set them on a tray; place into the freezer. Once frozen, transfer the balls to a zip-lock bag and freeze until ready to bake. Place cookies, straight from the freezer, onto a parchment-lined cookie sheet. They will need to bake a couple of minutes longer than non-frozen dough.

■ When making cookies that use mix-ins such as chocolate chips, don't hesitate to mix them up. Replace chocolate chips with flavored chips of your choice, such as butterscotch, peanut butter, cappuccino, or anything that will work well with the flavor. You can also add chopped nuts, dried fruits (diced small), or cereal, etc., for textural and flavor contrasts.

■ Do not overbake cookies! Many cookies, such as drop cookies, firm up as they cool. They may look too soft at the end of the stated baking time, but don't be tempted to bake your cookies longer, as that will ruin their texture.

Chocolate Pretzel
COOKIES

Dairy or **Pareve** | **Yield** about 3½ dozen

If you're familiar with my blog, you're probably familiar with one of its most popular recipes: Pretzel Crusted Chicken Fingers. They're a staple in my home (and in the homes of thousands of my readers). These cookies might have never happened if not for the leftover pretzel crumbs in my pantry. One day, I wanted to make chocolate cookies — but I was in the mood for a sweet and salty overload. I wanted to make sure that every bite was an indulgence and packed with flavor. I opened the pantry door and saw the pretzels — and these cookies immediately started to take shape in my brain. And that's why I keep extra pretzel crumbs in the pantry!

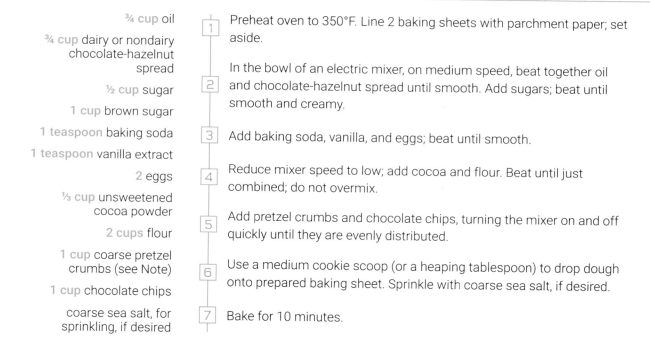

¾ cup oil

¾ cup dairy or nondairy chocolate-hazelnut spread

½ cup sugar

1 cup brown sugar

1 teaspoon baking soda

1 teaspoon vanilla extract

2 eggs

⅓ cup unsweetened cocoa powder

2 cups flour

1 cup coarse pretzel crumbs (see Note)

1 cup chocolate chips

coarse sea salt, for sprinkling, if desired

1. Preheat oven to 350°F. Line 2 baking sheets with parchment paper; set aside.

2. In the bowl of an electric mixer, on medium speed, beat together oil and chocolate-hazelnut spread until smooth. Add sugars; beat until smooth and creamy.

3. Add baking soda, vanilla, and eggs; beat until smooth.

4. Reduce mixer speed to low; add cocoa and flour. Beat until just combined; do not overmix.

5. Add pretzel crumbs and chocolate chips, turning the mixer on and off quickly until they are evenly distributed.

6. Use a medium cookie scoop (or a heaping tablespoon) to drop dough onto prepared baking sheet. Sprinkle with coarse sea salt, if desired.

7. Bake for 10 minutes.

Note Make pretzel crumbs by crushing pretzels in the food processor. Don't process them to a fine powder, though — you still want to have some pretzel texture in the cookies.

Variation Replace some or all of the chocolate chips with nougat chips for an extra burst of flavor.

Plan Ahead These cookies freeze well in an airtight bag or container.

Fruity Pebbles
COOKIES

Dairy or **Pareve** | **Yield** 3-4 dozen cookies

I call these good-aunt cookies, because I made these especially for my nieces. They're also practical cookies, because I had some Fruity Pebbles cereal that wasn't being eaten. Here's the surprise though — while these are obviously delicious and colorful for kids, grownups love them too, because they can't get enough of the amazing textural contrast between the chewy cookie and the crunchy cereal.

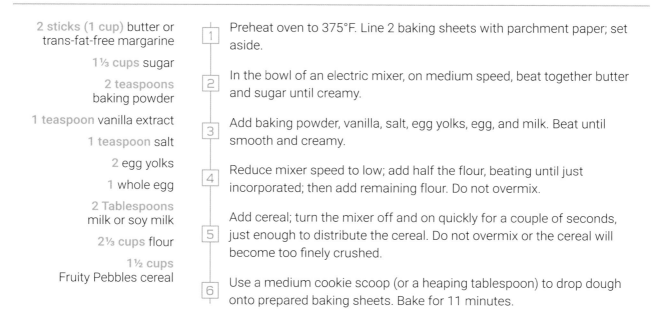

2 sticks (1 cup) butter or
trans-fat-free margarine

1⅓ cups sugar

2 teaspoons
baking powder

1 teaspoon vanilla extract

1 teaspoon salt

2 egg yolks

1 whole egg

2 Tablespoons
milk or soy milk

2⅓ cups flour

1½ cups
Fruity Pebbles cereal

1. Preheat oven to 375°F. Line 2 baking sheets with parchment paper; set aside.

2. In the bowl of an electric mixer, on medium speed, beat together butter and sugar until creamy.

3. Add baking powder, vanilla, salt, egg yolks, egg, and milk. Beat until smooth and creamy.

4. Reduce mixer speed to low; add half the flour, beating until just incorporated; then add remaining flour. Do not overmix.

5. Add cereal; turn the mixer off and on quickly for a couple of seconds, just enough to distribute the cereal. Do not overmix or the cereal will become too finely crushed.

6. Use a medium cookie scoop (or a heaping tablespoon) to drop dough onto prepared baking sheets. Bake for 11 minutes.

Note Using oil instead of butter or margarine will change the texture considerably. The cookies will be less chewy, but the flavor will remain the same.

Plan Ahead These cookies freeze well in an airtight container. The texture of these cookies is important, so for maximum enjoyment, defrost them completely before serving.

No-Margarine
CHOCOLATE CHIP COOKIES

Pareve | Yield **About 4 dozen**

It's always been important to me to listen to readers' requests and create recipes that they're going to like. (What can I say — I'm a people pleaser!) So when the requests for margarine-free cookie recipes came pouring in, I knew I had to listen. Did people appreciate the recipe? Did they like it? Well, after thousands of Ami Magazine readers raved about them, I put the recipe up on my blog, where it's been viewed (so far!) by almost a quarter of a million people! Whether you prefer to bake without butter or margarine, simply don't have it on hand, or just want to try something new, you'll be in good company when enjoying this recipe!

1 cup oil

1 cup brown sugar

½ cup sugar

2 teaspoons vanilla extract

1 teaspoon baking soda

1 teaspoon salt

2 eggs

2 Tablespoons cornstarch

2½ cups flour

1½ cups good-quality chocolate chips

1. Preheat oven to 375°F. Line 2 baking sheets with parchment paper; set aside.

2. In the bowl of an electric mixer, on medium speed, beat together oil and sugars until smooth and creamy.

3. Add vanilla, baking soda, salt, eggs, and cornstarch, beating well to combine after each addition. Reduce mixer speed to low. Add flour; beat until just combined. Add chocolate chips; stir until evenly distributed.

4. Using a medium cookie scoop (or a heaping tablespoon), drop dough onto prepared baking sheets. Bake for 8-9 minutes, until tops are set. Do not overbake.

Variation Instead of the chocolate chips, use the flavored chip of your choice, such as peanut butter, butterscotch, or nougat.

Plan Ahead These cookies freeze well in an airtight container or bag.

Chocolate Chunk
CHOCOLATE COOKIES

Pareve | **Yield** 3½-4 dozen cookies

This recipe was published in my column in Ami Magazine, just a couple of days before the big blizzard (that wasn't) in the New York area in 2015. Stuck at home with not much to do, everyone turned to bake … these cookies! Chewy, easy to make, and without any butter or margarine, these cookies are both delicious and irresistible. So many of my readers spent their snow day making these cookies that one of them quipped, "We should rename this from The Blizzard of 2015 to The Miriam Pascal Cookie Blizzard!"

1 cup oil

1 cup brown sugar

⅔ cup sugar

1 teaspoon vanilla extract

1 teaspoon baking soda

½ teaspoon baking powder

½ teaspoon salt

2 eggs

2 Tablespoons cornstarch

½ cup unsweetened cocoa powder

2 cups flour

10-12 ounces chocolate chips or chunks (see Note)

1. Preheat oven to 350°F. Line 2 baking sheets with parchment paper; set aside.

2. In the bowl of an electric mixer, on medium speed, beat together oil and sugars until combined.

3. Add vanilla, baking soda, baking powder, salt, and eggs. Beat until smooth.

4. Reduce mixer speed to low. Add cornstarch, cocoa, and flour. Beat until just combined — do not overmix.

5. Add chocolate chunks; stir until evenly distributed.

6. Use a medium cookie scoop (or a heaping tablespoon) to drop dough onto prepared baking sheets.

7. Bake for 10 minutes, until light golden brown.

Note For best results in any recipe using chocolate chips, start with a good-quality chocolate bar and chop it into chunks yourself. Don't hesitate to add more than the recipe calls for!

Variation Instead of chocolate chips, use the flavored chip of your choice, such as peanut butter, butterscotch, or nougat.

Plan Ahead These cookies freeze well in an airtight container or bag.

Trail Mix
OATMEAL COOKIES

Pareve | Yield 3½ dozen

These cookies have a wonderful flavor, but it's the texture that makes them particularly extraordinary. The cookies are crunchy on the outside and chewy on the inside. Add the various textures of the nuts, fruit (and candy!) in the trail mix, and you're in for a real treat.

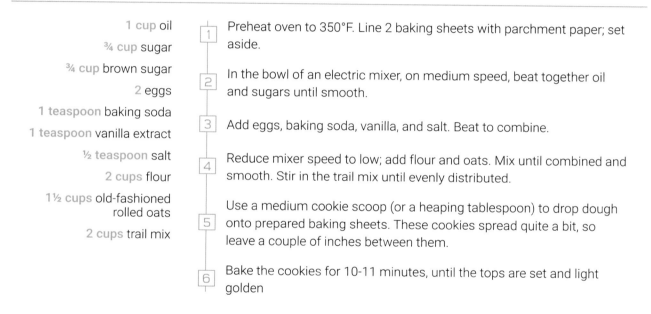

1 cup oil

¾ cup sugar

¾ cup brown sugar

2 eggs

1 teaspoon baking soda

1 teaspoon vanilla extract

½ teaspoon salt

2 cups flour

1½ cups old-fashioned rolled oats

2 cups trail mix

1. Preheat oven to 350°F. Line 2 baking sheets with parchment paper; set aside.

2. In the bowl of an electric mixer, on medium speed, beat together oil and sugars until smooth.

3. Add eggs, baking soda, vanilla, and salt. Beat to combine.

4. Reduce mixer speed to low; add flour and oats. Mix until combined and smooth. Stir in the trail mix until evenly distributed.

5. Use a medium cookie scoop (or a heaping tablespoon) to drop dough onto prepared baking sheets. These cookies spread quite a bit, so leave a couple of inches between them.

6. Bake the cookies for 10-11 minutes, until the tops are set and light golden

Note You can use your favorite purchased trail mix in these cookies, or create your own by combining your choice of nuts, raisins, and candies.

Variation For Oatmeal Butterscotch Cookies, use one cup butterscotch chips and one cup toasted chopped pecans in place of the trail mix.

Plan Ahead These cookies freeze well in an airtight container or bag.

Flourless Fudge
COOKIES

Pareve | Yield 2½ dozen

I'm not generally a gluten-free baker, but there are times when everyone needs a flourless recipe, such as when you're baking for your gluten-free friends or for Passover. I tried a ton of different flourless cookie recipes, trying to figure out which to include in this book. My criteria were very strict: I wouldn't include a cookie recipe that was "good enough." Even though it was flourless, it had to be as good as every other cookie in this chapter. Well, my friends, this is the one. It's devoid of flour, but perfectly delicious anyway.

½ cup nut butter (see Note)

½ cup oil

1½ cups sugar

2 eggs

1 teaspoon vanilla extract

1½ teaspoons baking powder

½ teaspoon salt

1 cup unsweetened cocoa powder

⅔ cup corn starch or potato starch

½ cup powdered sugar

1. Preheat oven to 350°F. Line 2 baking sheets with parchment; set aside.

2. In the bowl of an electric mixer, on medium speed, beat together nut butter and oil until smooth. Add sugar; beat until smooth and creamy.

3. Add eggs, vanilla, baking powder, and salt; beat until combined. Reduce mixer speed to low; add cocoa. Beat to combine. Add corn starch; beat until just combined.

4. Use a medium cookie scoop (or a heaping tablespoon) to portion out dough. Roll into balls; then roll in powdered sugar until fully coated. Place on prepared baking sheets. Bake for 10 minutes.

Notes ■ Use peanut, cashew, or almond butter, depending on taste and allergy restrictions. (Ashkenazic Jews do not use peanut butter on Passover.) ■ Some nuts have stronger flavor than others; peanut butter will impart a stronger flavor than cashew or almond butters.

Variation These are great without the powdered sugar as well. Simply skip the step of rolling the cookies in powdered sugar. Roll scoops of dough into balls and bake as instructed. Instead, sift powdered sugar over cookies after baking, as seen in the photo.

Plan Ahead These cookies freeze well in an airtight container or bag. Some of the powdered sugar may dissolve in the freezer, but the cookies will still taste the same.

Chocolate Chunk
HONEY COOKIES

Pareve | **Yield** about 3 dozen

If you're a fan of chocolate chip cookies and a fan of honey cookies, this combination of the two is right up your alley! These soft, chewy, and slightly cakey cookies have a distinct honey flavor, but also have those chocolate chips we all love!

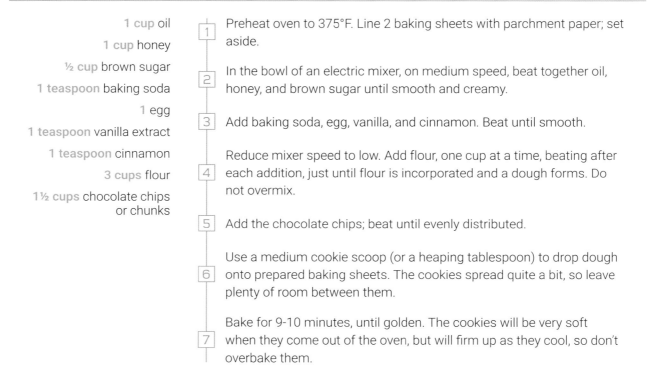

1 cup oil

1 cup honey

½ cup brown sugar

1 teaspoon baking soda

1 egg

1 teaspoon vanilla extract

1 teaspoon cinnamon

3 cups flour

1½ cups chocolate chips or chunks

1. Preheat oven to 375°F. Line 2 baking sheets with parchment paper; set aside.

2. In the bowl of an electric mixer, on medium speed, beat together oil, honey, and brown sugar until smooth and creamy.

3. Add baking soda, egg, vanilla, and cinnamon. Beat until smooth.

4. Reduce mixer speed to low. Add flour, one cup at a time, beating after each addition, just until flour is incorporated and a dough forms. Do not overmix.

5. Add the chocolate chips; beat until evenly distributed.

6. Use a medium cookie scoop (or a heaping tablespoon) to drop dough onto prepared baking sheets. The cookies spread quite a bit, so leave plenty of room between them.

7. Bake for 9-10 minutes, until golden. The cookies will be very soft when they come out of the oven, but will firm up as they cool, so don't overbake them.

Variation Use caramel or butterscotch chips in place of chocolate chips for a different flavor.

Plan Ahead These cookies freeze well in an airtight container. The texture of these cookies is important, so for maximum enjoyment, defrost them completely before serving.

Blueberry Muffin
COOKIES

Pareve | **Yield** 3-3½ dozen

These soft and summery cookies are an incredible hybrid of cookies and muffins, sharing both the perfect muffin taste and the cookie texture. Make them all year round using frozen blueberries, but be sure to follow the note carefully to avoid having the color run into your cookies.

¾ cup oil

⅔ cup sugar

⅔ cup brown sugar

1 teaspoon baking powder

½ teaspoon baking soda

½ teaspoon salt

2 teaspoons vanilla extract

2 eggs

1 cup cornmeal

2 cups flour

1½ cups blueberries, fresh or frozen (see Note)

1. Preheat oven to 375°F. Line 2 cookie sheets with parchment paper; set aside.

2. In the bowl of an electric mixer, on medium speed, cream together butter and sugars until smooth.

3. Add baking powder, baking soda, salt, and vanilla. Add eggs, one at a time, beating well to combine after each addition.

4. Reduce mixer speed to low. Add cornmeal; beat until combined. Add flour in two additions, beating after each addition until just combined.

7. Stir in blueberries, very gently, to prevent the colors from running.

8. Using a medium cookie scoop (or a heaping tablespoon), drop dough onto prepared baking sheets, leave 2-3 inches between cookies to allow spreading.

9. Bake for about 11-12 minutes, until the tops appear set.

Note If using frozen blueberries, defrost blueberries completely; this will take at least a couple of hours. Once they have defrosted, drain off all the accumulated liquid. Squeeze lightly to drain as much liquid from the berries as possible. Toss drained blueberries with 2 tablespoons flour.

Plan Ahead These freeze well in an airtight container. The cookies are quite soft, so layer them carefully on a flat surface between sheets of parchment paper before freezing.

Chocolate Peanut Butter
SANDWICH COOKIES

Dairy or **Pareve** | **Yield** about 20 sandwich cookies

Reading this cookbook, you will probably get a good idea of some of the flavors I enjoy, but I can't think of a flavor combination that I like more than chocolate and peanut butter. These fabulous cookies are packed with both of my favorite dessert flavors, and they're really pretty too.

1½ sticks (¾ cup) butter or trans-fat-free margarine

¾ cup creamy peanut butter

1 cup brown sugar

½ cup sugar

2 eggs

1 teaspoon vanilla extract

1 teaspoon baking soda

½ cup unsweetened cocoa powder

2 cups flour

½ cup peanut butter chips

½ cup chocolate chips

FILLING

1½ sticks (¾ cup) butter or trans-fat-free margarine

¾ cup creamy peanut butter

¾ cup marshmallow fluff

¾ cup powdered sugar

1. Preheat oven to 350°F. Line two baking sheets with parchment paper; set aside.

2. In the bowl of an electric mixer on medium speed, beat together butter, peanut butter, and sugars until creamy.

3. Add eggs, vanilla, and baking soda, beating well to combine after each addition.

4. Reduce mixer speed to low; add cocoa, then flour. Beat to combine. Stir in chips until evenly distributed.

5. Using a small cookie scoop (or a heaping teaspoon), drop dough onto prepared baking sheets. Bake for 8-9 minutes, until set. Allow to cool completely before filling.

6. **Prepare the filling:** In the bowl of an electric mixer fitted with the whisk attachment, on medium speed, beat together butter, peanut butter, and marshmallow fluff until smooth. Add sugar; beat until fluffy.

7. **Assembly:** Spoon or pipe the filling onto the flat side of a cookie; top with a second cookie.

Notes ■ Use all chocolate chips or all peanut butter chips, instead of a combination.
■ For the look in the photo, pipe on the filling using a piping bag fitted with a large star tip, such as a Wilton 1M tip.

Variation While the filling really takes these cookies over the top, they're also great as stand-alone cookies without the filling! Use a medium cookie scoop (instead of a small one) and bake them for an extra minute or two.

Plan Ahead The sandwiches can be frozen in an airtight container or bag, but you'll get better results if you freeze them without the filling. Make the filling and assemble the sandwiches up to one day before serving.

Tiramisu
COOKIES

Dairy or **Pareve** | **Yield** about 3½ dozen

Traditional tiramisu is a coffee-flavored dessert, noted for its ladyfingers soaked in espresso. I reinterpreted this fabulous dessert into cakey cookies, packed with coffee flavor and rolled in coffee-soaked ladyfinger crumbs.

CRUMBS

1 cup coarse ladyfinger crumbs

2 Tablespoons brown sugar

1 Tablespoon brewed coffee (or ½ teaspoon instant coffee granules dissolved in 1 Tablespoon hot water)

COOKIE DOUGH

¾ cup oil

4 ounces cream cheese or soy cream cheese

1 cup brown sugar

½ cup sugar

¼ cup espresso or strong coffee (see Note)

1 egg

1 teaspoon baking soda

½ teaspoon salt

1 teaspoon vanilla extract

3 cups flour

1. Preheat oven to 350°F. Line 2 baking sheets with parchment paper; set aside.

2. **Prepare the crumbs:** Combine ladyfinger crumbs, brown sugar, and coffee in a small bowl. Stir until combined. Mixture should have the texture of damp sand. Set aside.

3. **Prepare the cookie dough:** In the bowl of an electric mixer, on medium speed, beat together oil, cream cheese, and sugars until smooth.

4. Add espresso, egg, baking soda, salt, and vanilla. Beat until smooth and creamy.

5. Reduce mixer speed to low; add flour, one cup at a time, beating after each addition, until combined.

6. Use a medium cookie scoop (or a heaping tablespoon) to portion out dough. Roll into balls; then roll in prepared ladyfinger crumbs until fully coated. Place onto prepared baking sheets.

7. Bake for 10-11 minutes, until cookies are set.

Note You can use 2 teaspoons instant coffee granules dissolved in ¼ cup hot water instead of espresso.

Plan Ahead These cookies freeze well in an airtight container or bag. They're on the soft side, so handle with care when packing them. Defrost fully before serving.

Bourbon Pecan
SNOWBALL COOKIES

Dairy or **Pareve** | **Yield** about 4 dozen

"These taste like a grown-up version of a snowball cookie," said my sister-in-law Freidi after tasting one. That description is perfect! These elegant cookies are similar to those well-known cookies, but with a faint taste of bourbon. Don't worry about serving it to kids, though — the alcohol cooks off during the baking.

2 sticks (1 cup) butter or trans-fat-free margarine

¾ cup sugar

1 Tablespoon bourbon

1 teaspoon vanilla extract

¾ cup ground pecans

1¾ cups flour

¾ cup powdered sugar

1. Preheat oven to 375°F. Line 2 baking sheets with parchment paper; set aside.

2. In the bowl of an electric mixer, on medium speed, beat together butter and sugar until smooth.

3. Add bourbon, vanilla, and pecans. Beat to combine. Reduce mixer speed to low; add flour. Beat until incorporated and a smooth dough has formed.

4. Use a small cookie scoop (or a heaping teaspoon) to portion out dough; roll into balls. Place onto prepared baking sheets. The cookies will not spread much during baking, so you can bake them fairly close together.

5. Bake for 10 minutes. Remove from oven and immediately roll the cookies in powdered sugar, coating them completely.

Notes ■ If you don't have or don't want to use bourbon, you can substitute one additional teaspoon vanilla and two teaspoons water.
■ The butter or margarine is vital to the texture of these cookies, so do not replace with oil.

Plan Ahead These cookies freeze well in an airtight container or bag. The powdered sugar may dissolve when frozen, but you can sift additional powdered sugar over them just before serving.

Apple Pie
THUMBPRINT COOKIES

Dairy or **Pareve** | **Yield** about 5 dozen

These cookies are a great blend of the classic, all-American apple pie and that nostalgic cookie we all know and love. They have a fantastic, melt-in-your mouth texture, and the apple filling smells great — and tastes even better! Fuji and Honey Crisp apples work well in this recipe; however, any apples that are available will be fine.

3 sticks (1½ cups) butter or trans-fat-free margarine

1½ cups powdered sugar

2 teaspoons vanilla extract

1 egg white

3 cups flour

FILLING

3 large apples, peeled and shredded

2 teaspoons lemon juice

1 Tablespoon ground cinnamon

½ teaspoon ground ginger

⅓ cup brown sugar

1. Preheat oven to 375°F. Line 2 baking sheets with parchment paper; set aside.

2. In the bowl of an electric mixer, on medium speed, beat together butter, sugar, vanilla, and egg white until combined.

3. Reduce mixer speed to low; gradually add flour. Beat until dough forms.

4. **Prepare the filling:** Combine all filling ingredients in a small bowl; set aside.

5. Use a small cookie scoop (or a heaping teaspoon) to drop dough onto prepared baking sheets. Roll into balls; press down in the center of each ball, using your thumb or a teaspoon measuring spoon to make "thumbprints." Drain the liquid from the bowl of filling; discard liquid. Place about ¾ teaspoon drained filling into the indentation of each cookie.

6. Bake for 10-11 minutes, until the cookies begin to turn golden.

Note You can use oil in place of butter or margarine in this recipe, but the dough will be harder to work with and a bit crumbly. The cookies will still taste great, though.

Variation In place of the apple filling, you can use canned pie filling of your choice. Simply spoon a small amount into each cookie.

Plan Ahead These cookies freeze well. Store them in a pan or container with parchment paper between the layers.

Gingerbread
BISCOTTI

Pareve | Yield 30 biscotti

One of the things I love to do with desserts and baked goods is to take a familiar flavor that people know and enjoy (say, gingerbread) and merge it with a type of dessert where you don't usually find said flavor — in this case, biscotti. It's a creative twist, but one that doesn't leave you wondering if you'll like it.

⅓ cup oil

⅓ cup sugar

⅓ cup brown sugar

⅓ cup molasses

2 eggs

1½ teaspoons cinnamon

1½ teaspoons ginger

½ teaspoon nutmeg

1 teaspoon baking powder

1 teaspoon baking soda

½ teaspoon salt

2⅓ cups flour

¾ cup white chocolate chips

1. Preheat oven to 350°F. Line two baking sheets with parchment paper; set aside.

2. In the bowl of an electric mixer, on medium speed, combine oil, sugars, molasses, and eggs. Beat until smooth and creamy. Add cinnamon, ginger, nutmeg, baking powder, baking soda, and salt. Beat to combine.

3. Turn the mixer speed to low; add flour. Beat to combine. Add white chocolate chips; stir until evenly distributed.

4. Form the dough into two long logs. It is easiest to do this with slightly damp hands. Place each one onto prepared baking sheet. Each log should take up most of the length of the cookie sheet.

5. Bake for 28 minutes; set aside to cool for about 10 minutes.

6. Slice the log into diagonal slices about ½-inch wide. Lay the slices, cut side up, on the baking sheet; bake for 7 minutes. Turn slices over; bake an additional 7-8 minutes.

Plan Ahead These biscotti freeze well in an airtight container or bag.

Lemon Olive Oil
BISCOTTI

Pareve | **Yield** 15 large biscotti

While olive oil isn't a standard baking ingredient, when used correctly, the flavor can really enhance your baked goods. One of my favorite flavor pairings for olive oil is lemon (and other citrus flavors). These cookies have an amazing (but subtle) fruity flavor, thanks to this lovely flavor combination.

¾ cup extra virgin or light olive oil

¾ cup sugar

zest of 1 lemon

2 Tablespoons lemon juice

1 teaspoon vanilla extract

1½ teaspoons baking powder

pinch salt

2 eggs

2¼ cups flour

1 Preheat oven to 350°F. Line a baking sheet with parchment paper; set aside.

2 In the bowl of an electric mixer, on medium speed, beat together olive oil, sugar, and lemon zest until smooth. Add lemon juice, vanilla, baking powder, salt, and eggs. Beat until combined and creamy.

3 Add flour; beat on low until just combined. The dough will be loose and sticky.

4 Form the dough into a long, narrow log along the length of the prepared baking sheet (it will spread along the width, so don't make it too wide). It is easiest to do this with slightly damp hands. Bake for 25 minutes. Remove from the oven; allow to cool for about 5 minutes.

5 Slice the log into diagonal slices about ½-inch wide. Lay the slices, cut side up, on the baking sheet; bake for 15 minutes. Turn slices over; bake an additional 10 minutes.

Plan Ahead
These biscotti freeze well in an airtight container or bag.

No-Margarine
SUGAR COOKIES

Pareve | **Yield** about 3 dozen

My readers quite frequently request recipes that don't use margarine (or butter). And among the most common requests is one for a sugar cookie. It was a tough challenge, because the margarine (or butter) is integral to the texture of the cookie and helps maintain its shape. This recipe required more tests than any other in the book, but when I finally got it right, I was ready to jump for joy. The numerous test batches were all worth it, because I know that so many people will be thrilled to try this recipe.

¾ cup oil

1½ cups sugar

1 egg

2 egg yolks

2 teaspoons vanilla extract

2⅓ cups flour

1. In the bowl of an electric mixer, on medium speed, beat together oil and sugar until combined. Add egg, egg yolks, and vanilla; beat until creamy.

2. Reduce mixer speed to low; add flour, about one third at a time. Beat after each addition only until the flour is mixed in and soft dough forms. Do not overmix.

3. Preheat oven to 350°F. Line a baking sheet with parchment paper; set aside.

4. On a lightly floured surface, roll dough to about ¼-inch thickness. Using cookie cutters or the rim of a glass, cut dough into desired shapes; place on prepared baking sheet. Cookies do not spread much, so you can place them fairly close together.

5. Bake for 11-13 minutes, or until the edges are light golden brown. Remove from oven; set aside to cool completely before decorating, if desired (see Note).

Notes ■ Decorate with Royal Icing (page 186), or with any of the glazes on pages 190-193. ■ You can also decorate with rolled fondant. Roll the fondant very thin, then cut with the same cutter as the cookie; "glue" it to the cookie by brushing a thin layer of corn syrup or honey on the cookie and pressing the fondant onto it.

Plan Ahead These cookies freeze well in an airtight container or bag. If freezing them after decorating, it's best to store them between layers of parchment paper. Note that frozen decorations may become discolored. These cookies can also be kept, airtight, at room temperature for at least one week.

Chocolate Cheesecake
PINWHEEL COOKIES

Dairy or **Pareve** | **Yield** about 4 dozen

These cookies are deceptively fancy. They look really pretty, but the dough and filling are super-easy to make. And let me tell you — these aren't just about their looks! With a soft, chewy texture and an amazingly flavorful filling, you'll find these to be as delicious as they are pretty.

DOUGH

2 sticks (1 cup) butter or trans-fat-free margarine

1 cup sugar

4 egg yolks

2 teaspoons baking powder

½ teaspoon salt

1½ teaspoons vanilla extract

2 Tablespoons milk or soy milk

2¾ cups flour

FILLING

4 ounces semisweet chocolate, melted and cooled

4 ounces cream cheese or soy cream cheese

1. In the bowl of an electric mixer, on medium speed, beat together butter and sugar until combined.

2. Add egg yolks, baking powder, salt, vanilla, and milk. Beat until smooth. Add flour, half at a time, beating after each addition until a smooth dough forms.

3. Prepare the filling: Combine the chocolate and cream cheese in a small bowl; stir until smooth. Set aside.

4. On a lightly floured surface, roll half the dough into a rectangle about 12 inches by 16 inches. Spread half the filling over the dough, then roll it up tightly along the long side.

5. Place roll onto a tray; repeat with remaining dough and filling. Place tray with rolls into the freezer; chill until firm, at least 1 hour.

6. Preheat oven to 350°F. Line 2 baking sheets with parchment paper; set aside.

7. Cut rolls into slices about one-third-inch thick. Place slices cut side up on prepared baking sheets. Leave about a half-inch between slices to allow for spreading.

8. Bake for 10-12 minutes, until cookies are just set. They'll still be a bit soft when they come out of the oven, so don't handle them until they cool.

Note Don't be tempted to skip the step of freezing the logs, or the pinwheel shape will become misshapen while you're slicing them.

Variations ■ Oil can replace butter here, but the dough will be harder to work with. ■ This dough makes great hamantaschen! See page 198 in Holiday Guide.

Plan Ahead Cookies freeze well in an airtight container. These cookies are on the softer side, so store in a pan or sturdy container, to keep them from breaking.

Fudgy
BROWNIES

Pareve | **Yield** about 2 dozen

There are tons of ways to make delicious brownies, but I am a fan of the easiest method: using cocoa powder. That's right, no melted chocolate, no multiple bowls. These brownies are dense and fudgy — a chocolate lover's dream — and they're amazingly easy to make!

4 eggs

2 cups sugar

1 cup oil

1 teaspoon vanilla extract

½ teaspoon salt

1½ cups unsweetened cocoa powder

1 cup flour

1. Preheat oven to 325°F. Grease a 9x13-inch pan well; set aside.

2. In the bowl of an electric mixer, on medium speed, beat together eggs, sugar, oil, vanilla, and salt until smooth.

3. Reduce mixer speed to low. Add cocoa, then flour, beating to combine after each addition. The batter will be very thick and fudgy.

4. Pour batter into prepared pan; gently smooth top with a spatula.

5. Bake for 30-35 minutes, until the top is just set. Remove from oven and set aside to cool before cutting into 2-inch squares.

Note Brownies are pretty much a blank slate for frostings and glazes, so take your pick from the options on pages 188-193.

Variation For brownie bites, grease a mini muffin pan well. Fill cups three-quarters full with brownie batter. Bake for 10-11 minutes.

Plan Ahead These brownies freeze well in an airtight container or bag. For best results, freeze whole; cut into squares just before serving.

Oatmeal
COOKIE WEDGES

Dairy or **Pareve** | **Yield** 2 dozen

There's an old joke: "Oatmeal raisin cookies that look like chocolate chip cookies are the main reason I have trust issues." Jokes aside, these versatile cookies work with (c)raisins (if you like those), chocolate chips (if that's your preference), and lots of other flavors. Baking these in wedges instead of as traditional drop cookies means you don't have to scoop out the dough, which saves a lot of time.

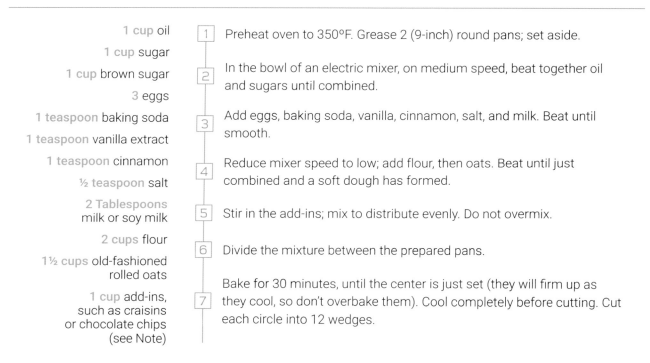

1 cup oil

1 cup sugar

1 cup brown sugar

3 eggs

1 teaspoon baking soda

1 teaspoon vanilla extract

1 teaspoon cinnamon

½ teaspoon salt

2 Tablespoons milk or soy milk

2 cups flour

1½ cups old-fashioned rolled oats

1 cup add-ins, such as craisins or chocolate chips (see Note)

1 | Preheat oven to 350°F. Grease 2 (9-inch) round pans; set aside.

2 | In the bowl of an electric mixer, on medium speed, beat together oil and sugars until combined.

3 | Add eggs, baking soda, vanilla, cinnamon, salt, and milk. Beat until smooth.

4 | Reduce mixer speed to low; add flour, then oats. Beat until just combined and a soft dough has formed.

5 | Stir in the add-ins; mix to distribute evenly. Do not overmix.

6 | Divide the mixture between the prepared pans.

7 | Bake for 30 minutes, until the center is just set (they will firm up as they cool, so don't overbake them). Cool completely before cutting. Cut each circle into 12 wedges.

Note These wedges are extremely versatile. Mix in craisins, chocolate chips, butterscotch or caramel chips, nuts, or any combination you like. I love butterscotch and pecans!

Variation Dip ends in melted chocolate for a pretty presentation.

Plan Ahead These freeze well in an airtight container or bag.

Cookies 'n Cream
BARS

Dairy or **Pareve** | **Yield** 12-14 servings

Cookies 'N Cream Ice Cream is a fabulous flavor, but why let ice cream have all the fun? These easy-to-make bars are really exceptional — mostly thanks to the flavor and texture of the crushed cookies that are mixed in!

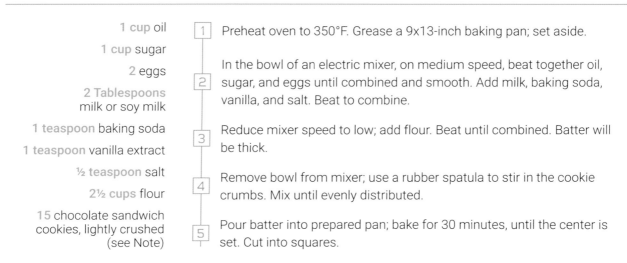

1 cup oil

1 cup sugar

2 eggs

2 Tablespoons milk or soy milk

1 teaspoon baking soda

1 teaspoon vanilla extract

½ teaspoon salt

2½ cups flour

15 chocolate sandwich cookies, lightly crushed (see Note)

1. Preheat oven to 350°F. Grease a 9x13-inch baking pan; set aside.

2. In the bowl of an electric mixer, on medium speed, beat together oil, sugar, and eggs until combined and smooth. Add milk, baking soda, vanilla, and salt. Beat to combine.

3. Reduce mixer speed to low; add flour. Beat until combined. Batter will be thick.

4. Remove bowl from mixer; use a rubber spatula to stir in the cookie crumbs. Mix until evenly distributed.

5. Pour batter into prepared pan; bake for 30 minutes, until the center is set. Cut into squares.

Note There's no need to crush the cookies in a food processor, as you want small pieces, not crumbs. Place the cookies into a plastic bag within a second bag. Crush them with a heavy pan or rolling pin — you should see pieces and crumbs of varying sizes.

Variation Top with Vanilla Glaze (page 190) or Chocolate Glaze (page 191).

Plan Ahead These bars can be frozen in an airtight container. For best results, freeze whole; cut into squares just before serving.

■ People often worry about taking their bundt cakes out of the pan without breaking them, but a few easy tricks will ensure success!

[1] **GREASE THE PAN WELL.** Don't skimp on the nonstick spray and make sure to spray all the way up the sides of the pan, as well as the tube.

[2] **FLOUR YOUR PAN.** You can purchase floured nonstick spray (often called Baking Spray), or you can coat the pan in a thin layer of flour by sprinkling a small amount of flour over the surface of the greased pan, then shake it off carefully to remove all excess.

[3] **LET IT COOL.** Don't try to remove the cake until it has had some time to cool. For best results, flip it over after 15 minutes of cooling.

[4] **LOOSEN THE CAKE.** Gently run a flexible utensil (I often use a plastic knife or thin spatula) around the inner edge of the pan to separate the cake from the pan. As you flip the cake over a plate, feel for any resistance as it comes out. If necessary, instead of hitting the pan to force the cake out, turn it back over and run the utensil between the pan and the area that is stuck. Then try again, turning pan over to remove the cake.

CAKE AND CUPCAKES

- If a cake over-bakes or breaks when you take it out the pan, you can salvage the pieces by crumbling them and layering them in a dish with one of the mousse recipes (pages 128-136) to create a beautiful trifle.

- Turn any of the bundt cakes into mini bundt cakes by dividing the batter among the cups of a mini bundt pan. On average, the mini cakes will need about half the baking time of the full-size cake, but check for doneness a few minutes before the halfway mark, to avoid over-baking.

- For best results when baking bundt cakes, use good-quality, non-disposable pans. The tips above for removing cakes from the pan have been tested with Nordic Ware nonstick pans. Additionally, pay attention to the shape. Some of the more complex shaped pans make cake removal harder.

- Piping frosting nicely onto your cupcakes is easy when you have the right tip. I recommend a large star tip. A popular shape (used in much of the piping you see in this cookbook) is the Wilton 1M tip. For a beautiful swirl, start at the edge of the cupcake, then swirl the frosting around the edge, forming smaller swirls as you go around until it ends in a point.

Snickerdoodle
BUNDT CAKE

Dairy or **Pareve** | **Yield** 12-15 servings

Traditional Snickerdoodles are a favorite in my house. The soft, pillowy cookies are amazing, but that cinnamon-sugar crust is what really makes them special! I decided to create a cake version of this popular treat by giving this super-easy, cinnamony cake a coating similar to the crust on those favorite cookies.

¾ cup oil

1 cup sugar

1 cup brown sugar

5 eggs

1 teaspoon vanilla extract

1 teaspoon cinnamon

1 teaspoon baking soda

1 teaspoon
baking powder

2 cups flour

½ cup milk or soy milk

COATING

3 Tablespoons sugar

1 Tablespoon cinnamon

1. Prepare the coating: Combine sugar and cinnamon in a small bowl.

2. Preheat oven to 350°F. Coat a standard (12-cup) bundt pan well with nonstick spray or oil (see Note), making sure to cover the entire pan.

3. Sprinkle one third of the coating into the prepared pan, making sure to cover the outer surface of the tube as well.

4. In the bowl of an electric mixer, on medium speed, beat together oil and sugars until combined.

5. With the mixer running, add eggs, one at a time, beating after each addition until creamy. Beat in vanilla, cinnamon, baking soda, and baking powder.

6. Reduce mixer speed to low; add half the flour, followed by the milk, beating to combine after each addition. Beat in remaining flour.

7. Pour half the batter into the pan; top with one third of the coating. Cover with remaining batter. Top with remaining coating.

8. Bake for 45 minutes, or until a tester inserted into the center comes out clean. Allow cake to cool for 10-15 minutes before removing from pan.

Note If using oil instead of nonstick spray to grease the pan, it's easiest to use a pastry brush to brush the oil over every part of the inside of the pan, including the tube.

Plan Ahead This cake freezes well when stored airtight. Wrap cake in foil and then seal it in a zip-lock bag.

Strawberries and Cream
BUNDT CAKE

Dairy or **Pareve** | **Yield** 12-15 servings

This is one of the first recipes I ever came up with on my own. After it was published in my column in Ami Magazine, it was also my first recipe to ever "go viral." It was an instant favorite with my family — and my readers. Nobody can get enough of the somewhat unusual strawberry flavor — or the light, fluffy texture. This was way back in the beginning of my food writing career, but even then, I thought … maybe I'll write a cookbook some day and include this cake recipe in it.

½ cup heavy whipping cream or nondairy whip

4 eggs

1¾ cups sugar

1 teaspoon vanilla extract

1 teaspoon strawberry extract

2-3 drops red food coloring (optional, but recommended)

½ cup oil

½ cup strawberry purée (see Note)

2 cups flour

1 (4-oz) package instant vanilla pudding mix

1 Tablespoon baking powder

Vanilla Glaze (page 190), optional

1. Preheat oven to 350°F. Coat a standard (12-cup) bundt pan with floured baking spray. Coat well to ensure the cake unmolds easily.

2. In the bowl of an electric mixer, on high speed, whip cream until stiff. Use a rubber spatula to remove whipped cream to a small bowl; set aside. No need to wash bowl before continuing to next step.

3. In the same mixer bowl, on medium speed, beat together eggs and sugar until smooth and creamy, about 2 minutes. Add vanilla, strawberry extract, and food coloring, if using. Stir on low speed to combine.

4. Add oil and puréed strawberries. Beat to combine. Add flour, pudding mix, and baking powder; stir just to combine. Use a rubber spatula to gently fold in reserved whipped cream.

5. Pour batter into prepared pan; bake for 40-45 minutes, until a tester inserted into the center comes out clean.

6. Allow cake to cool for 10-15 minutes before removing from pan.

7. Set cake aside to cool completely before topping with Vanilla Glaze, if desired.

Note This cake works really well with frozen strawberries, so you can easily make it all year round. To purée strawberries: Completely defrost frozen strawberries; purée in food processor until smooth. You'll need about 1 cup whole frozen strawberries to make ½ cup purée.

Plan Ahead This cake freezes well when stored airtight. Wrap cake in foil and then seal it in a zip-lock bag. It's best to freeze it without the glaze; add glaze just before serving.

Brown Sugar Rum
BUNDT CAKE

Dairy or **Pareve** | **Yield** 12-15 servings

I originally came up with this cake during a seemingly endless winter in New York. The weather was cold and snowy, but when I tasted this cake, the flavors transported me, at least for a minute, to a tropical beach.

⅔ cup oil

1½ cups brown sugar

½ cup sugar

4 eggs

⅓ cup rum

1 teaspoon baking soda

1 teaspoon baking powder

½ teaspoon salt

2 teaspoons vanilla extract

2 cups flour

½ cup milk or soy milk

Vanilla Glaze or **Brown Sugar Glaze** (page 190), optional

1. Preheat oven to 350°F. Grease and flour a standard (12-cup) bundt pan; set aside.

2. In the bowl of an electric mixer, on medium speed, beat together oil and sugars until combined.

3. Add eggs, rum, baking soda, baking powder, salt, and vanilla. Beat until combined and smooth.

4. Reduce mixer speed to low. Add half the flour, followed by the milk, followed by remaining flour. Beat after each addition until just combined.

5. Pour batter into prepared pan.

6. Bake for 45-50 minutes, until a tester inserted into the center comes out clean. Allow cake to cool for 10-15 minutes before removing from pan. Set aside to cool completely before glazing.

7. Top with Vanilla Glaze or Brown Sugar Glaze, optional.

Variation To make Pineapple Rum Bundt Cake, stir 1 cup of well-drained pineapple chunks into the batter before baking.

Plan Ahead This cake freezes well when stored airtight. Wrap cake in foil and then seal it in a zip-lock bag. It's best to freeze it without the glaze; add glaze just before serving.

Caramel Apple
BUNDT CAKE

Dairy or **Pareve** | **Yield** 12-15 servings

For me, the consolation of summer being over has always been the fresh apples appearing in stores. And while we can't always eat those apples in the favorite way of our childhood — on a stick, coated in gooey caramel — the good news is that this cake will bring back the flavors of that childhood treat. The tartness of Granny Smith apples makes them best in this recipe.

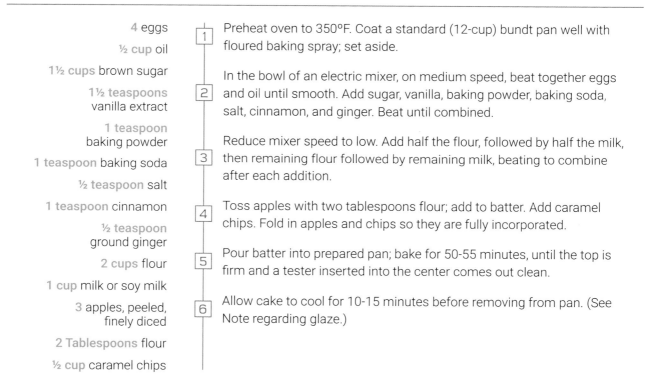

4 eggs

½ cup oil

1½ cups brown sugar

1½ teaspoons vanilla extract

1 teaspoon baking powder

1 teaspoon baking soda

½ teaspoon salt

1 teaspoon cinnamon

½ teaspoon ground ginger

2 cups flour

1 cup milk or soy milk

3 apples, peeled, finely diced

2 Tablespoons flour

½ cup caramel chips

1 Preheat oven to 350°F. Coat a standard (12-cup) bundt pan well with floured baking spray; set aside.

2 In the bowl of an electric mixer, on medium speed, beat together eggs and oil until smooth. Add sugar, vanilla, baking powder, baking soda, salt, cinnamon, and ginger. Beat until combined.

3 Reduce mixer speed to low. Add half the flour, followed by half the milk, then remaining flour followed by remaining milk, beating to combine after each addition.

4 Toss apples with two tablespoons flour; add to batter. Add caramel chips. Fold in apples and chips so they are fully incorporated.

5 Pour batter into prepared pan; bake for 50-55 minutes, until the top is firm and a tester inserted into the center comes out clean.

6 Allow cake to cool for 10-15 minutes before removing from pan. (See Note regarding glaze.)

Note The cake is quite sweet and really delicious all on its own, so you might prefer it without a glaze. If you do glaze it, use Vanilla Glaze (page 190) or Cinnamon Spice Glaze (page 191), but let cake cool completely before glazing.

Plan Ahead This cake freezes well when stored airtight. Wrap cake in foil and then seal it in a zip-lock bag. It's best to freeze it without the glaze; add glaze just before serving.

Peanut Butter & Banana Chocolate Chip
BUNDT CAKE

Dairy or **Pareve** | **Yield** 12-15 servings

This cake has many different flavors going on, but they complement each other in the most amazing way! If you've got over-ripe bananas on your counter, this is a great way to make sure they don't go to waste. Best of all? This cake is really easy to make!

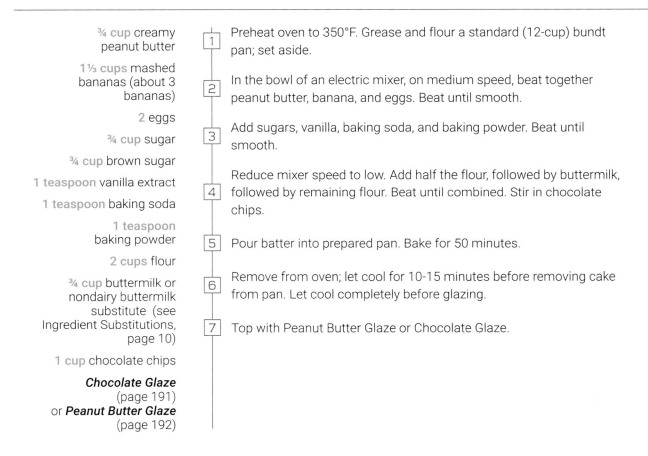

¾ cup creamy peanut butter

1⅓ cups mashed bananas (about 3 bananas)

2 eggs

¾ cup sugar

¾ cup brown sugar

1 teaspoon vanilla extract

1 teaspoon baking soda

1 teaspoon baking powder

2 cups flour

¾ cup buttermilk or nondairy buttermilk substitute (see Ingredient Substitutions, page 10)

1 cup chocolate chips

Chocolate Glaze (page 191) or **Peanut Butter Glaze** (page 192)

1. Preheat oven to 350°F. Grease and flour a standard (12-cup) bundt pan; set aside.

2. In the bowl of an electric mixer, on medium speed, beat together peanut butter, banana, and eggs. Beat until smooth.

3. Add sugars, vanilla, baking soda, and baking powder. Beat until smooth.

4. Reduce mixer speed to low. Add half the flour, followed by buttermilk, followed by remaining flour. Beat until combined. Stir in chocolate chips.

5. Pour batter into prepared pan. Bake for 50 minutes.

6. Remove from oven; let cool for 10-15 minutes before removing cake from pan. Let cool completely before glazing.

7. Top with Peanut Butter Glaze or Chocolate Glaze.

Variation Sub peanut butter chips for all or half the chocolate chips.

Plan Ahead This cake freezes well when stored airtight. Wrap cake in foil and then seal it in a zip-lock bag. It's best to freeze it without the glaze; add glaze just before serving.

Fluffy Chocolate
BUNDT CAKE

Dairy or **Pareve** | **Yield** 12-15 servings

One of my goals when writing this book was to include all of those "basic" recipes — those that aren't flashy but are simple to make and are staples that we all need to have up our sleeves. I believe that a simple, flavorful, chocolate bundt cake is the perfect example of this style of recipe. Pull out this recipe when a simple chocolate cake is just what you need.

¾ cup oil

2 cups sugar

4 eggs

1 teaspoon vanilla extract

½ teaspoon salt

1½ teaspoons baking powder

1 teaspoon baking soda

¾ cup unsweetened cocoa powder

1½ cups flour

1 cup milk or soy milk

Glaze (see Note)

1. Preheat oven to 350°F. Grease and flour a standard (12-cup) bundt pan; set aside.

2. In the bowl of an electric mixer, on medium speed, combine oil, sugar, and eggs; beat until creamy.

3. Add vanilla, salt, baking powder, and baking soda. Beat until combined.

4. Reduce mixer speed to low; add cocoa and half the flour; beat until combined. Add milk and remaining flour; beat until smooth. Do not overmix.

5. Pour batter into prepared pan. Bake for 45-50 minutes, or until a tester inserted into the center comes out clean.

6. Allow cake to cool for 10-15 minutes before removing from pan. Set aside to cool completely before glazing, optional (see Note).

Note This cake goes well with any of the frostings and glazes on pages 188-193.

Variation This cake may be baked in a 9x13-inch pan for 50-55 minutes. Do not bake as cupcakes; for chocolate cupcakes, see page 86.

Plan Ahead This cake freezes well when stored airtight. Wrap cake in foil and then seal it in a zip-lock bag. It's best to freeze it without the glaze; add glaze just before serving.

Ultimate Vanilla
BUNDT CAKE

Dairy or **Pareve** | **Yield** 12-15 servings

It's a shame that people consider vanilla desserts to be lacking in any real flavor, when vanilla actually has a distinct — and exceptionally good — taste all on its own! To create the Ultimate Vanilla Bundt Cake, I wanted a cake that was not only bursting with this amazing flavor, but was also light and fluffy and easy to make. This is a basic recipe, but a great one to have in your repertoire.

1 Tablespoon lemon juice

1 cup milk or soy milk

½ cup canola oil

4 eggs

1¾ cups sugar

1 (4-oz) package instant vanilla pudding mix

1 Tablespoon vanilla extract

1 teaspoon baking soda

1 teaspoon baking powder

2 cups flour

1. Preheat oven to 350°F. Grease and flour a standard (12-cup) bundt pan; set aside.

2. In a small bowl, combine lemon juice and milk; set aside while you prepare the rest of the batter. Mixture should curdle a bit.

3. In the bowl of an electric mixer, on medium speed, combine oil and eggs; beat lightly to combine.

4. Add sugar; beat on medium speed for a minute or two until slightly thickened.

5. Add pudding mix, vanilla, baking soda, and baking powder; beat to incorporate.

6. Add half the flour, followed by half the milk mixture, followed by the remainder of the flour and then the remainder of the milk, beating after each addition until batter is smooth. Do not overmix.

7. Pour batter into prepared pan. Bake for 45 minutes, or until a tester inserted into the center comes out clean. (See Note regarding glaze.)

Note This veratile cake works well with any frosting or glaze on pages 188-193. Cool cake for 10-15 minutes before removing from pan; cool completely before glazing.

Variations ■ To make a 9x13-inch sheet cake, bake for 50-55 minutes. ■ To make cupcakes, bake full-size cupcakes for 20 minutes or mini cupcakes for 14 minutes.

Plan Ahead This cake freezes well when stored airtight. Wrap the cake in foil and then seal it in a zip-lock bag. It's best to freeze it without the glaze; add glaze just before serving.

Triple Citrus
BUNDT CAKE

Pareve | **Yield** 12-15 servings

"Bursting with flavor!" That's the first thought that came to mind when I tasted the batter. Then I put the cake into the oven, and my kitchen was filled with the most incredible citrus aromas. The end result was even better than I could have hoped — and well worth the few extra minutes it takes to zest the fresh fruit.

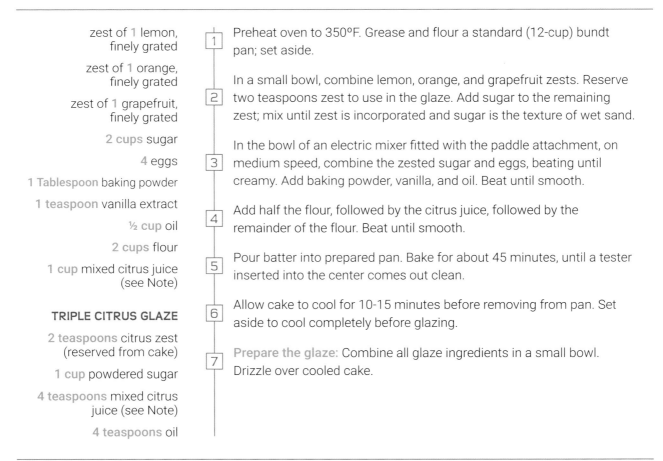

zest of **1** lemon, finely grated

zest of **1** orange, finely grated

zest of **1** grapefruit, finely grated

2 cups sugar

4 eggs

1 Tablespoon baking powder

1 teaspoon vanilla extract

½ cup oil

2 cups flour

1 cup mixed citrus juice (see Note)

TRIPLE CITRUS GLAZE

2 teaspoons citrus zest (reserved from cake)

1 cup powdered sugar

4 teaspoons mixed citrus juice (see Note)

4 teaspoons oil

1. Preheat oven to 350°F. Grease and flour a standard (12-cup) bundt pan; set aside.

2. In a small bowl, combine lemon, orange, and grapefruit zests. Reserve two teaspoons zest to use in the glaze. Add sugar to the remaining zest; mix until zest is incorporated and sugar is the texture of wet sand.

3. In the bowl of an electric mixer fitted with the paddle attachment, on medium speed, combine the zested sugar and eggs, beating until creamy. Add baking powder, vanilla, and oil. Beat until smooth.

4. Add half the flour, followed by the citrus juice, followed by the remainder of the flour. Beat until smooth.

5. Pour batter into prepared pan. Bake for about 45 minutes, until a tester inserted into the center comes out clean.

6. Allow cake to cool for 10-15 minutes before removing from pan. Set aside to cool completely before glazing.

7. Prepare the glaze: Combine all glaze ingredients in a small bowl. Drizzle over cooled cake.

Note After zesting the fruits, squeeze out their juices to use in both the cake and the glaze. If you can't squeeze enough juice from the fruit for both the cake and the glaze, add bottled juice to make up the difference.

Plan Ahead This cake freezes well, wrapped airtight. Although glazes are usually better made fresh, this one is easiest made at the same time as the cake because it uses some of the zest and juice, so glaze it before freezing. Let the glaze on the cake harden before you wrap it.

Honey Sour Cream
POUND CAKE

Dairy or **Pareve** | **Yield** 12-15 servings

Some people think of honey cake as something to bake once a year, just for Rosh Hashanah. But the flavor of honey is excellent in cakes, and this one has the most amazing, dense, and moist texture that it's important to let go of this notion and put this delicious and easy cake into your regular rotation of family favorites.

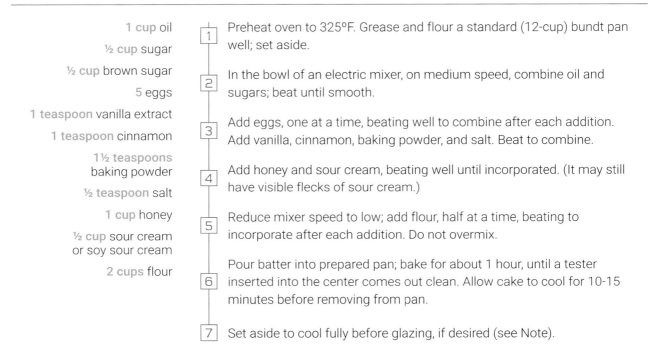

1 cup oil

½ cup sugar

½ cup brown sugar

5 eggs

1 teaspoon vanilla extract

1 teaspoon cinnamon

1½ teaspoons baking powder

½ teaspoon salt

1 cup honey

½ cup sour cream or soy sour cream

2 cups flour

1. Preheat oven to 325ºF. Grease and flour a standard (12-cup) bundt pan well; set aside.

2. In the bowl of an electric mixer, on medium speed, combine oil and sugars; beat until smooth.

3. Add eggs, one at a time, beating well to combine after each addition. Add vanilla, cinnamon, baking powder, and salt. Beat to combine.

4. Add honey and sour cream, beating well until incorporated. (It may still have visible flecks of sour cream.)

5. Reduce mixer speed to low; add flour, half at a time, beating to incorporate after each addition. Do not overmix.

6. Pour batter into prepared pan; bake for about 1 hour, until a tester inserted into the center comes out clean. Allow cake to cool for 10-15 minutes before removing from pan.

7. Set aside to cool fully before glazing, if desired (see Note).

Note This cake is great without a glaze, but a glaze really takes it over the top. I like to use Citrus Glaze (page 193), Cinnamon Spice Glaze (page 191), or Honey Glaze (page 193).

Variation For a different flavor, substitute 1 cup pure maple syrup or molasses for the honey. If using molasses, add a teaspoon of ground ginger, which complements the molasses well.

Plan Ahead This cake freezes well when stored airtight. Wrap cake in foil and then seal it in a zip-lock bag. It's best to freeze it without the glaze; add glaze just before serving.

Lemon Marble
POUND CAKE

Dairy or **Pareve** | **Yield** about 18 servings

This cake is for my father. I originally planned on sharing a recipe for a classic lemon pound cake, but then I remembered an Italian cake that my father loves. It was a dense pound cake, with a lemon flavor and chocolate marbled throughout. I didn't know where to find that original recipe, so I created my own based on my memories of it. The look on my father's face when I gave him a piece to taste was absolutely priceless — and you'll understand what all the fuss is about when you try this cake yourself.

1 cup oil

2 cups sugar

5 eggs

zest of 2 lemons, finely grated

¼ cup lemon juice

½ teaspoon baking soda

½ teaspoon baking powder

½ teaspoon salt

1 teaspoon vanilla extract

3 cups flour

¼ cup milk or soy milk

4 ounces semisweet chocolate, melted and cooled

1. Preheat oven to 350°F. Grease 2 (9-inch) loaf pans well; set aside.

2. In the bowl of an electric mixer, on medium speed, beat together oil, sugar, and eggs until creamy. Add zest, juice, baking soda, baking powder, salt, and vanilla. Beat to combine.

3. Reduce mixer speed to low; add half the flour, followed by the milk, followed by remaining flour; beat until combined.

4. Remove 2 cups of batter to a small bowl. Stir in melted chocolate until smooth.

5. Divide batters equally between prepared pans, alternating flavors. For the marbled effect, swirl a knife gently through the batters.

6. Bake for 50-55 minutes, until a tester inserted into the center comes out clean.

Variation For a bundt cake, bake in a standard (12-cup) bundt pan for 50-55 minutes.

Plan Ahead This cake freezes well in an airtight container or bag.

Carrot
POUND CAKE

Dairy or **Pareve** | **Yield** 8-10 servings

Carrots serve an important function in baked goods: They make you feel good — like you're eating your veggies! Joking aside, carrots add amazing flavor and texture to this cake, and I used whole wheat flour and less oil, to help with the lightened-up feel. Despite its lightness, it's still totally delicious!

¾ cup oil

½ cup brown sugar

½ cup sugar

2 eggs

1 teaspoon vanilla extract

1 cup finely grated carrots (about two large carrots)

½ teaspoon baking soda

1½ teaspoons baking powder

½ teaspoon salt

1 teaspoon cinnamon

2½ cups white whole wheat flour

¾ cup milk or soy milk

Cream Cheese Glaze (p. 191), optional

1. Preheat oven to 350°F. Grease a 9-inch loaf pan; set aside.

2. In the bowl of an electric mixer fitted with the paddle attachment, on medium speed, beat together oil and sugars until smooth. Beating well to combine after each addition, add eggs, vanilla, carrots, baking soda, baking powder, salt, and cinnamon.

3. Reduce mixer speed to low; add half the flour, followed by the milk, then the remaining flour, beating until just combined.

4. Pour batter into prepared loaf pan; bake for 60-65 minutes. Remove from oven; set aside to cool completely before glazing.

5. Drizzle glaze over cooled cake, if desired.

Note If you're trying to cut calories, omit the glaze. The cake is great without it, too!

Plan Ahead This cake freezes well when stored airtight. Wrap cake in foil and then seal it in a zip-lock bag. It's best to freeze it without the glaze; add glaze just before serving.

S'mores
CRUMB CAKE

Dairy or **Pareve** | **Yield** about 18 servings

When debating with myself which blog recipes to include in this cookbook, I was stuck on my S'mores Bundt Cake. It's completely delicious — and very popular — largely because it's easy to make but also strikingly pretty. Eventually, I decided to adapt my own recipe, and I came up with this variation: dense chocolate cake on the bottom, a thick layer of graham cracker crumbs on top, and little toasted marshmallow surprises mixed in.

CRUMBS

1 sleeve graham crackers, coarsely crushed (just under 2 cups)

½ cup brown sugar

1 cup flour

½ cup oil

¾ cup mini marshmallows

BATTER

5 eggs

⅔ cup oil

1 cup sugar

1 cup brown sugar

1 teaspoon baking powder

1 teaspoon baking soda

½ teaspoon salt

1 teaspoon vanilla extract

½ cup unsweetened cocoa powder

¾ cup milk or soy milk

1¾ cups flour

1. Preheat oven to 350°F. Grease a 9x13-inch baking pan; set aside.

2. Prepare the crumbs: In a small bowl, stir together crushed graham crackers, brown sugar, and flour. Add oil; mix until crumbs form. Add marshmallows; stir to distribute.

3. Prepare the batter: In the bowl of an electric mixer, on medium speed, beat together eggs, oil, and sugars until smooth.

4. Add baking powder, baking soda, salt, and vanilla. Mix until combined.

5. Reduce mixer speed to low; add cocoa, followed by milk, then flour, beating after each addition until incorporated. Do not overmix.

6. Pour batter into prepared baking pan. Distribute crumb mixture evenly over the batter.

7. Bake for 55-65 minutes, until a tester inserted into the center comes out clean. Allow cake to cool completely before cutting.

Note It's easy to prepare the cracker crumbs in a food processor, but you want texture in the topping, with some crumbs and some larger pieces, so don't over-process. Place the graham crackers into a plastic bag within a second bag. Crush them with a heavy pan or rolling pin — you should see pieces and crumbs of varying sizes.

Plan Ahead This cake freezes well in an airtight container.

Note You can replace fresh peaches with frozen peach slices, fully defrosted and drained.

Variation In place of peaches, use apple slices for a fall-inspired version of the cake.

Plan Ahead This cake will stay fresh for a couple of days in the refrigerator. It can be frozen in an airtight container or bag, but it is best fresh.

Chocolate Celebration
CAKE

Dairy or **Pareve** | **Yield** about 16 servings

While most of the recipes in this book tend more toward the easy-to-make side, I decided that I had to include one great layer cake to celebrate special occasions. I have always been a fan of Hershey's classic chocolate layer cake, and in this recipe, I've taken that basic cake and kicked it up a notch by adding extra richness and flavor. Customize this cake by using your favorite frosting flavor.

2 cups sugar

2 eggs

½ cup oil

2 teaspoons vanilla extract

1½ teaspoons baking powder

1½ teaspoons baking soda

1 teaspoon salt

⅔ cup unsweetened cocoa powder

1¾ cups flour

1 cup milk or soy milk

6 oz semisweet chocolate, melted and cooled

1 cup brewed coffee (or 1 Tablespoon instant coffee dissolved in 1 cup boiling water)

2 batches frosting of your choice (pages 188-189)

sprinkles, chocolate shavings, or other garnishes, optional

1. Preheat oven to 350°F. Line 2 (9-inch) round pans with circles of parchment paper. Grease the pans and liners well; set aside.

2. In the bowl of an electric mixer, on medium speed, beat together sugar, eggs, and oil until smooth.

3. Add vanilla, baking powder, baking soda, and salt. Beat to combine.

4. Reduce mixer speed to low. Add cocoa, followed by half the flour, followed by the milk, then remaining flour, beating after each addition. Stir in melted chocolate and coffee until smooth.

5. Divide the batter between prepared pans. Bake for 30-35 minutes, until a tester inserted into the center comes out clean. Let cakes cool completely before frosting.

6. Assemble the cake: Place 4 strips of parchment paper around the edges of a turntable or cake stand to catch any drips as you work. Remove strips just before serving to present the cake neatly. Center one cake on the turntable. Spread a layer of frosting (about half-inch thick) on the cake, then place the second cake upside down over it.

7. Spread a very thin layer of frosting over the surface of the entire cake, top and sides, to seal in the crumbs. It's not a problem if crumbs are in this layer of frosting or it isn't perfectly smooth, as it will be covered. Place the cake in the fridge for about an hour, to allow the frosting to firm up somewhat.

8. Pipe or spread the rest of the frosting over the top and sides of the cake. If desired, decorate with sprinkles, chocolate shavings, or other garnishes.

Note To create the rose look in the photo, pipe roses of frosting along the sides of the cake. Start at the bottom, work your way up the sides, then fill in the top. To pipe a rose, use a piping bag fitted with a large star tip (such as a Wilton 1M). Starting at the center, hold the bag at a 90-degree angle to the cake; squeeze the frosting out clockwise around the center, forming the rose.

Variation Pipe the frosting in swirls over the cake or simply spread over cake and decorate with chocolate shavings or sprinkles.

Plan Ahead You can make the cake layers ahead and freeze them. Once assembled, the cake can be stored in the fridge for up to a few days.

Orange Creamsicle
CUPCAKES

Dairy or **Pareve** | **Yield** 2 dozen

Remember orange creamsicle pops? The creamy ice cream mixed with a burst of orange flavor is a nostalgic memory for me — and probably for you as well. In these cupcakes, I tried to capture the best of that treat — the orange and cream flavor combination — without the chemical aftertaste and the sticky fingers. These cupcakes may scream summer, but they're bound to brighten any day of the year!

1½ **cups** sugar

zest of **1** orange, finely grated

1 cup oil

4 eggs

½ **teaspoon** salt

1 Tablespoon baking powder

3 cups flour

1¼ **cups** orange juice

Cream Cheese Frosting
(page 191)

1 Preheat oven to 350°F. Line 2 standard (12-cup) cupcake pans with paper liners; set aside.

2 In the bowl of an electric mixer, on medium speed, combine sugar and orange zest until mixture resembles the texture of wet sand. Add oil, eggs, salt, and baking powder, beating well to combine after each addition.

3 Add half the flour, followed by half the juice; then remaining flour, followed by remaining juice, beating after each addition until just combined.

4 Spoon batter into prepared pans, filling each cup about three-quarters full.

5 Bake for 15-18 minutes, until tops are set. Remove from oven; set aside to cool completely before frosting.

6 Spread or pipe frosting onto cooled cupcakes.

Note To make a high mound of frosting (as shown in the photo), double the frosting recipe.

Variation For mini cupcakes, bake in mini cupcake pans for about 9 minutes, or until set.

Plan Ahead The cupcakes freeze well in an airtight container or bag. For best results, freeze them without the frosting; frost them just before serving.

Pomegranate
CUPCAKES

Pareve | **Yield** 1 dozen

Pomegranates are beautiful fruits, loaded with health benefits and delicious flavors, so it's a shame they aren't used more in baking! These easy-to-make and unusual cupcakes have a delicate fruity flavor and pretty pink appearance, thanks to the glaze.

½ cup oil

¾ cup sugar

1 teaspoon vanilla extract

½ teaspoon salt

½ teaspoon baking soda

1 teaspoon baking powder

2 eggs

1½ cups flour

½ cup pomegranate juice

POMEGRANATE GLAZE

1½ cups powdered sugar

2-3 Tablespoons pomegranate juice, divided

pomegranate seeds, for garnish, optional

1. Preheat oven to 350°F. Line a standard (12-cup) cupcake pan with paper liners; set aside.

2. In the bowl of an electric mixer, on medium speed, beat together oil and sugar until smooth and creamy.

3. Add vanilla, salt, baking soda, baking powder, and eggs. Beat until combined.

4. Alternately add half the flour and half the pomegranate juice, beating after each addition until incorporated.

5. Spoon batter into prepared pan, filling each cup about three-quarters full.

6. Bake for 16-18 minutes, until the tops are set. Remove from oven; cool completely before glazing.

7. Prepare the glaze: In a small bowl, combine powdered sugar with 2 tablespoons pomegranate juice; mix until smooth. Gradually add an additional 1-3 teaspoons juice if needed to form a thick but spreadable glaze.

8. Dip the tops of the cooled cupcakes into the glaze, allowing excess to drip back into the bowl. Garnish with pomegranate seeds, if desired.

Variation The flavors of pomegranate and chocolate go really well together, so you can frost these with Chocolate Fudge Frosting (page 188).

Plan Ahead These cupcakes freeze well in an airtight container. For best results, freeze them without the glaze and add it just before serving, but you can glaze them before freezing if necessary. Be sure to let the glaze set before you cover the cupcakes.

Chocolate and Strawberry *CUPCAKES*

Dairy or **Pareve** | **Yield** 1 dozen

My 7-year-old niece Miri is already a budding baker. She loves to bake with me, and suggested we make cupcakes together. I let her choose the type she wanted, and after deliberating, she came up with this recipe idea. "Let's make chocolate cupcakes with strawberry frosting!" These look pretty (and perfect for a little girl), and they taste even better than they look.

CUPCAKES

½ cup oil

1 cup sugar

2 eggs

1 teaspoon vanilla extract

½ teaspoon salt

1 teaspoon baking powder

½ teaspoon baking soda

⅓ cup unsweetened cocoa powder

1¼ cups flour

½ cup milk or soy milk

FROSTING

2 sticks (1 cup) butter or trans-fat-free margarine

½ cup smooth strawberry jam or preserves

1 teaspoon vanilla extract

½ teaspoon lemon juice

1-2 drops red food coloring, optional but recommended

1½ cups powdered sugar

1. Preheat oven to 350°F. Line a standard (12-cup) cupcake pan with paper liners; set aside.

2. In the bowl of an electric mixer, on medium speed, beat together oil, sugar, and eggs until creamy. Add vanilla, salt, baking powder, and baking soda. Beat until incorporated.

3. Reduce mixer speed to low; add cocoa and flour. Beat until mostly incorporated. Add milk; beat until smooth. Do not overmix.

4. Spoon batter into prepared pan, filling each cup about three-quarters full.

5. Bake for 17-20 minutes, until the tops feel set and somewhat firm. Set aside to cool completely before frosting.

6. Prepare the frosting: In the bowl of an electric mixer fitted with the whisk attachment, on medium speed, beat together butter, jam, vanilla, lemon juice, and food coloring (if using) until smooth.

7. Reduce mixer speed to low; add sugar. Beat until smooth and fluffy. Pipe or spoon frosting onto cooled cupcakes.

Note To make a high mound of frosting (as shown in the photo), double the frosting recipe.

Variations ■ Instead of the strawberry frosting, use your choice of frosting from pages 188-189, such as Chocolate Fudge or Salted Caramel Frosting. ■ Bake mini cupcakes for about 11 minutes.

Plan Ahead These cupcakes freeze well in an airtight container. Frosting keeps in an airtight container in fridge for about a week. For best results, freeze without frosting; add frosting just before serving.

■ If using bulk-packed yeast, note that one packet of dry yeast contains 2¼ teaspoons.

■ When frying (such as the Bakery Style Cake Donuts on page 104), place a piece of carrot in the oil to prevent the oil from burning. You'll notice the carrot get darker and darker, but the oil won't burn.

■ Muffin batters need to be gently mixed, so avoid over-mixing them. The good news about this is that muffins are easily made without a mixer.

■ People often assume that due to their similar looks, muffins and cupcakes are pretty much the same. However, muffins are generally less sweet, denser, and slightly drier than cupcakes. Because they aren't as sweet as cupcakes, muffins make a great breakfast to grab when you're on the go.

MUFFINS *AND* PASTRIES

Fruit Crumb
MUFFINS

Dairy or **Pareve** | **Yield** 18 muffins

A muffin should be dense, with the perfect amount of fruit or other fillings. There should definitely be a crumb topping. These muffins have it all. Amazing texture. Sweet, but not too sweet. And they're very versatile, so you can turn them into blueberry muffins in the spring and summer, apple muffins in the fall and winter, and chocolate chip muffins in between.

BATTER

2 eggs

½ cup oil

½ cup milk or soy milk

1 teaspoon vanilla extract

1 cup sugar

½ teaspoon salt

2 teaspoons baking powder

2¼ cups flour

1 mix-in (see below)

TOPPING

⅓ cup sugar

⅔ cup brown sugar

1 cup flour

2 teaspoons ground cinnamon

¼ cup oil

1. **Prepare the batter:** Preheat oven to 375°F. Line standard muffin pans with paper liners; set aside.

2. In a medium bowl, whisk together eggs, oil, milk, and vanilla until smooth.

3. Add sugar, salt, baking powder, and flour. Using a sturdy spoon, mix until combined. Add **one** mix-in option of your choice. Stir until evenly distributed.

4. Divide batter among the prepared cups, filling each about three-quarters full; set aside.

5. **Prepare the topping:** Combine all topping ingredients in a small bowl; mix until crumbs form.

6. Sprinkle topping over the prepared muffins. Bake for 17-19 minutes, until the tops are set.

MIX-IN OPTIONS

1 cup fresh or frozen blueberries (not defrosted)

2 large apples, peeled and finely diced

3 ripe peaches, peeled and finely diced

1 cup fresh or frozen cherries, pitted and quartered

1 cup chocolate chips

Variation These muffins can be made in mini muffin pans instead of full-size pans. Bake mini muffins for 8-9 minutes. Yield: 35-40 mini muffins.

Plan Ahead These muffins freeze well in an airtight container or bag.

Healthy Mocha
MUFFINS

Dairy or **Pareve** | **Yield** 16-18 standard muffins or 48-54 mini muffins

These muffins make a great breakfast! Not only are they packed with coffee flavor, but they're on the healthful side, so you can feel good about the food choices that start your day.

½ cup unsweetened applesauce

¼ cup agave syrup or honey

¼ cup oil

2 eggs

1 teaspoon vanilla extract

½ cup strong coffee

½ cup milk or soy milk

1½ teaspoons baking soda

1½ teaspoons baking powder

2 cups whole wheat flour or white whole wheat flour

2 Tablespoons unsweetened cocoa powder

½ cup old-fashioned rolled oats

½ cup Splenda (12 packets), sugar, or other dry sweetener

¾ cup chocolate chips, regular or sugar-free (optional)

1. Preheat oven to 375°F. Line standard muffin pans or mini muffin pans with paper liners; set aside.

2. In a medium bowl, whisk together applesauce, agave syrup, and oil until smooth. Add eggs, vanilla, coffee, milk, baking soda, and baking powder. Whisk until combined.

3. Add flour, cocoa, oats, and Splenda. Using a large spoon, stir the mixture until all the dry ingredients are incorporated and the mixture is smooth. Stir in chocolate chips, if using.

4. Spoon the batter into prepared pans, filling each cup about half full.

5. Bake standard muffins for 15 minutes or minis for 9-10 minutes, or until the tops are set.

Plan Ahead These muffins freeze well in an airtight container or bag.

Healthy Apple Spice
MUFFINS

Dairy or **Pareve** | **Yield** 16-18 muffins

Of all of the great aromas that come out of a kitchen, none are as enticing as those we associate with fall baking: cinnamon, ginger, nutmeg …. The flavors of fall are warm and comforting, and always difficult to resist. But these muffins are lightened up and don't contain lots of unhealthy ingredients, so there's no need to resist them.

½ cup unsweetened (natural) applesauce

¼ cup oil

¼ cup agave syrup or honey

1 teaspoon vanilla extract

1½ teaspoons cinnamon

½ teaspoon ground ginger

¼ teaspoon nutmeg

1 teaspoon baking soda

1 teaspoon baking powder

⅓ cup Splenda (8 packets), sugar, or other dry sweetener

2 eggs

1 cup (skim) milk or soy milk

2 apples, peeled and very finely diced

2 cups white whole wheat flour

1. Preheat oven to 350°F. Line standard muffin pans with paper liners; set aside.

2. In a large mixing bowl, whisk together applesauce, oil, and agave syrup until smooth.

3. Add vanilla, cinnamon, ginger, nutmeg, baking soda, baking powder, and Splenda. Whisk to combine. Add eggs and milk; whisk to combine.

4. Using a wooden spoon, stir in apples. Add flour; stir until incorporated.

5. Spoon mixture into prepared pans, filling the cups almost full.

6. Bake for 16-18 minutes, or until tops are set.

Variation Substitute blueberries or finely diced peaches for the apples to bake a summer-inspired version of these muffins.

Plan Ahead These muffins are best fresh from the oven, but you can freeze them. Keep them in an airtight container or bag. Freeze them by ones or twos in small zip-lock bags, and grab a bag for breakfast on-the-go.

93

Grandma's Sweet Yeast
DOUGH

Dairy or **Pareve** | **Yield** 2¼ pounds

When trying out various yeast doughs to include in my cookbook, I worked out some that were good, but none had that "wow" factor. That's when my mother reminded me that her mother a"h was a legendary baker, and that her Sticky Buns were most famous of all of her treats. My Aunt Nancy was kind enough to find my grandmother's recipes and send me a scanned copy of Grandma's handwritten recipe. My grandmother was elderly and quite ill by the time I was born, but it felt so special to connect with her through this recipe. This dough has an amazing texture and fabulous flavor, and I'm sure she would have been so proud to know that it's being published here, and that your family will enjoy it too.

1 package (2¼ teaspoons or ¼ ounce) dry yeast

1 cup lukewarm milk or soy milk

pinch sugar

½ cup flour

½ cup oil

½ cup sugar

2 eggs

3½ cups flour

1. In a small bowl, stir together yeast, milk, pinch sugar, and ½ cup flour. Set aside in a warm place until bubbles form.

2. Meanwhile, in the bowl of an electric mixer, on medium speed, beat together oil and ½ cup sugar until smooth.

3. Add eggs, one at a time, beating to combine after each addition.

4. Switch to the dough hook; reduce mixer speed to low. Add half the flour, followed by half the milk mixture, followed by the remaining flour and then remaining milk mixture. Knead at low speed until combined; then beat for an additional 5 minutes, until dough is smooth and elastic.

5. Coat the surface of the dough with nonstick cooking spray to prevent it from developing a hard crust. Cover bowl with a towel; set aside to rise in a warm place for about an hour and a half, or until dough has doubled in bulk.

6. Use this dough to make Fruit-Filled Pastry Roses (page 96), Cinnamon Cheese Buns (page 98), or your favorite recipe requiring yeast dough.

Variation Grandma's handwritten recipe indicates that she would add grated lemon rind (zest) to the dough before adding the flour. I left it out in the recipe because the dough is delicious even without it, but the extra burst of flavor is incredible, if you're inclined to add it.

Plan Ahead This dough is best used within a few hours of making it, but the treats you make with it can often be frozen (see following pages for details). For best results when serving yeast treats that have been frozen, reheat and serve them warm.

FRUIT-FILLED
Pastry Roses

Dairy or **Pareve** | **Yield** about 3 dozen

I was at my friend Liviya's house for Shabbos when I first saw this beautiful pastry shape in a magazine. The original recipe used a savory filling, and I instantly knew I had to come up with my own take on this gorgeous presentation. I tried it with a few different fillings, but Liviya is the one who gave me this beautiful — and very easy — idea. Don't be intimidated by the idea of making this shape — it's much easier than it looks!

1 batch Grandma's Sweet Yeast Dough (page 94)

FILLING

¾ **cup** smooth fruit preserves (see Note)

1 egg, lightly beaten

1. Preheat oven to 350°F. Line 2 baking sheets with parchment paper; set aside.

2. On a lightly floured surface, roll out one third of the dough as thin as possible into a rectangle about 12 inches by 16 inches.

3. Spread one third of the fruit preserves over the entire dough.

4. Cut the dough into thin strips ¾-1-inch wide and 16 inches long. Twist each strip by holding one end in each hand and twisting in opposite directions.

5. Coil a twist of dough around itself to form the rose shape. Tuck the end under the rose. Place on baking sheet and repeat with remaining dough. Leave 1½-2 inches between the roses, as they will expand while baking.

6. Repeat with remaining dough and preserves.

7. **Prepare the egg wash:** Using a fork, lightly beat egg with a spoonful of preserves. It does not need to be completely smooth. Brush over roses.

8. Bake for 13-15 minutes, until lightly golden.

Note For the prettiest look, use dark fruit preserves, such as strawberry, for strong contrast.

Variations ■ Use chocolate spread in place of the fruit filling. ■ For easier preparation, simply roll dough strips into pinwheels.

Plan Ahead Roses freeze well in an airtight container. Reheat defrosted roses at 350°F in a single layer on a baking sheet for a couple of minutes until warmed through. Serve immediately.

Cinnamon
CHEESE BUNS

Dairy or **Pareve** | **Yield** 2 dozen

When you think of a comfort food pastry, do you think of cinnamon buns? I know I do! The smell, the flavor, the texture … they're something to crave when you want homey comfort food. Instead of traditional cinnamon buns, I've taken these up a notch by adding cheese to the mix.

1 batch Grandma's Sweet
Yeast Dough (page 94)

8 oz cream cheese or
soy cream cheese

½ cup dark brown sugar

1½ Tablespoons
ground cinnamon

1 teaspoon vanilla extract

1 egg, lightly beaten

1 Combine cream cheese, brown sugar, cinnamon, and vanilla in a small bowl. Set aside.

2 Grease a 9x13-inch baking pan; set aside.

3 Divide dough into three equal parts. Working with one portion at a time, on a lightly floured surface, roll out the dough as thin as possible into a large rectangle, about 12 inches by 16 inches.

4 Spread one third of the cheese mixture over the dough. Roll the dough tightly along the short edge to form a roll about 12 inches long.

5 Cut the roll into 8 portions, each about 1½-inches wide. Place each bun, cut side up, side by side into the prepared pan. Repeat with remaining portions of dough. Allow buns to rise in the pan for 30-60 minutes, until the edges start to touch. Brush the tops with beaten egg.

6 Heat oven to 375°F. Bake for 30 minutes, then lower heat to 325°F; bake for an additional 8-10 minutes, until the tops are golden brown.

7 Serve warm, with glaze (see Note) if desired.

Variations
■ For Chocolate Cheese Buns, use a mixture of 4 ounces cream cheese and 4 ounces melted chocolate. ■ For Traditional Cinnamon Buns, instead of cream cheese filling, brush the dough with ½ cup oil, then top with a mixture of ½ cup sugar and 1 tablespoon cinnamon. Roll up and slice as directed.

Note
These are great unglazed, but you can use Cream Cheese Glaze (page 191) or Vanilla Glaze (page 190), to really take them over the top.

Plan Ahead
These freeze well in an airtight container. Defrost; reheat at 350°F just before serving; serve warm. Add glaze before serving.

Cream Cheese
RUGELACH

Dairy or **Pareve** | **Yield** 4 dozen

Shavuos might just be my favorite food holiday. I mean, it's a holiday whose customs dictate the eating of cheesecake and other dairy delights — who wouldn't love that? Of all the amazing treats I've made over the years, these Cream Cheese Rugelach, as simple as they may seem, stand out as a family favorite. Every year, my father gets a dreamy look in his eyes as he asks, "Will you please make me those amazing Cream Cheese Rugelach again this year?"

2 sticks (1 cup) butter or trans-fat-free margarine

8 oz cream cheese or soy cream cheese

⅓ cup sugar

2 egg yolks

½ teaspoon salt

1 teaspoon vanilla extract

3 cups flour

⅓ cup oil

FILLING

½ cup ground walnuts

½ cup sugar

1 teaspoon cinnamon

1 | In the bowl of an electric mixer, on medium speed, beat together butter and cream cheese until smooth.

2 | Add sugar, egg yolks, salt, and vanilla. Beat until creamy.

3 | Reduce mixer speed to low. Add the flour, half at a time; beat after each addition until combined and a smooth dough forms. Place dough into the refrigerator for a couple of hours, until firm enough to roll.

4 | Preheat oven to 350°F. Line 2 baking sheets with parchment paper; set aside.

5 | **Prepare the filling:** Combine nuts, sugar, and cinnamon in a small bowl; set aside.

6 | Divide the dough into thirds. On a lightly floured surface, roll one portion of dough into a large circle, about 15 inches in diameter. Brush the surface of the entire circle with one third of the oil, then sprinkle one third of the nut mixture over the entire surface.

7 | Cut the circle into 16 equal wedges. Working with one wedge at a time, roll it up (as tightly as possible), starting from the wider end and ending at the point. Place seam side down onto prepared pan. Repeat with remaining dough and filling.

8 | Bake for 16-18 minutes, until the rugelach are just starting to turn golden in color.

Note When made with nondairy margarine and soy cream cheese, these are delicious and still have the delicate, flaky texture. However, try them with butter and real cream cheese for an out-of-this-world flavor combination and a truly memorable treat.

Variation In place of the nut mixture, use chocolate-hazelnut spread or fruit preserves as the filling.

Plan Ahead Rugelach freeze well in an airtight container or bag. For best results, defrost and reheat at 350°F just before serving.

Healthy Chocolate
RUGELACH

Dairy or **Pareve** | **Yield** about 4 dozen, depending on size

There's something so homey about yeast dough and any goodies made with it. And while I won't claim that this is healthier than abstaining from dessert completely, I will assure you that you can enjoy the flavor and texture of this reduced calorie — and reduced guilt — option, even when watching the calories you eat and serve to your family.

DOUGH

1 packet (¼ oz or 2¼ teaspoons) dry yeast

¼ cup warm water

1 Tablespoon sugar

¼ cup milk or soy milk

¼ cup water

⅓ cup oil

½ cup honey or agave syrup

2 eggs

4 cups white whole wheat flour

FILLING

½ cup oil

½ cup honey or agave syrup

½ cup unsweetened cocoa powder

¾ cup sugar substitute, such as Splenda

1. In the bowl of an electric mixer, stir together yeast, water, and sugar. Let it sit for a couple of minutes until the mixture starts to bubble.

2. Add milk, water, oil, honey, eggs, and half the flour; beat to combine.

3. Switch to the dough hook; add remaining flour. Knead on low speed until a smooth dough forms. Knead for an additional five minutes.

4. Set dough aside to rise for one and a half hours, until doubled in bulk.

5. Prepare the filling: Combine all filling ingredients in a small bowl; whisk until smooth.

6. Preheat oven to 350°F. Line 2 baking sheets with parchment paper, set aside.

7. Divide dough into three parts. Working with one part at a time, roll the dough into a large circle — the thinner you roll it, the better the rugelach will be. Spread a quarter of the filling over the surface of the circle.

8. Cut circle into 16 wedges, then roll each wedge up, starting with the wider end and ending at the point. Place seam side down on prepared baking tray. Repeat with remaining dough and filling.

9. Bake for 16-18 minutes, until rugelach are just starting to turn golden.

Variation For Pinwheels, divide dough into thirds. Roll each third into a large rectangle. The thinner you roll it, the better. Spread with one third of filling. Roll up tightly along the long side; cut into 1-inch slices. Place slices cut side up onto parchment paper-lined baking sheets. Bake for 15 minutes.

Plan Ahead These freeze well in an airtight container or bag. Defrost and reheat at 350°F for a few minutes before serving.

Bakery Style
CAKE DONUTS

Dairy or **Pareve** | **Yield** 18-20 donuts

If you read "cake donut" and think "baked donut," think again. These donuts are made using a dough similar to cake batter, which utilizes baking powder instead of yeast to rise, so if you're intimidated by yeast (and even if you're not), you'll appreciate the simplicity of this recipe. My favorite thing about these donuts (as opposed to yeast donuts) is that while best freshly fried, these donuts stay fresher longer than yeast donuts, and they will still be great the next day!

2 eggs

¾ cup sugar

1 Tablespoon baking powder

¼ teaspoon nutmeg

1 teaspoon vanilla extract

3¾ cups flour

¾ cup milk or soy milk

¼ cup oil

oil, for frying

Glaze, optional
(see pages 190-193)

1. In the bowl of an electric mixer, on medium speed, beat together eggs and sugar until smooth and creamy, 2-5 minutes. Add baking powder, nutmeg, and vanilla; beat to combine.

2. Reduce mixer speed to low. Add one-third of the flour, followed by the milk, followed by another third of the flour; add oil, then remaining flour. Beat until a sticky dough forms. Refrigerate dough until firm, 1-2 hours or up to overnight.

3. Remove dough from the fridge (the dough will not rise until it is fried). Place it on a heavily floured surface. The dough will still be somewhat sticky, so it's important to use plenty of flour to roll it out.

4. Roll dough out to about ¼-inch thickness. Using a cookie cutter or the rim of a glass, cut out dough circles; then, with a smaller cutter or glass, cut a small circle from the center. Carefully pick up each donut to make sure it retains its shape. Reserve the small circles to fry as donut holes (see Variation).

5. Heat about 2 inches of oil in a medium saucepan or deep fryer over medium heat. Test the oil by dipping a donut into the oil; when ready, it will start to bubble immediately.

6. Fry 2 or 3 donuts at a time. Wait until you see the golden brown color start to creep up the side of the center before turning donuts. This will take about 1 to 1½ minutes. Flip the donuts and fry until golden brown on the other side, about a minute.

7. Remove from oil; drain on a paper towel-lined plate. Allow to cool slightly before glazing, optional.

Note I like to serve these donuts on a "donut bar." Prepare a variety of glazes (pages 190-193); present them in small cups or jars. Set out a variety of sprinkles, cookie crumbs, chopped nuts, and other toppings. Serve the donuts and let your guests enjoy creating their own flavor combinations.

Variation To make Cinnamon-Sugar Donut Holes: Combine 4 teaspoons sugar with 1 teaspoon cinnamon. Fry the small dough circles in hot oil for about 30 seconds per side. Remove from oil and roll hot donut holes in sugar mixture. Set aside to cool.

Plan Ahead These donuts are best fresh from the pan, and should ideally be eaten within the first few hours; however, they are still great the next day. Do not freeze.

■ Because butter or margarine used in making pie crusts should be frozen before use, I like to keep a couple of sticks in my freezer at all times, so I don't need to plan ahead when making pie crust.

■ While frozen fruit allows you to make out-of-season pies all year long, always look for the in-season fruits for tastiest pies.

■ The pies in this section offer various shaping suggestions (such as lattice or hand pies), but don't be afraid to switch it up. Use the filling you like best with the shape or method that appeals to you most.

PIES *AND* TARTS

■ To make pie crust cookies, roll
out pie dough as if you're baking
a pie, then cut into strips or use a
cookie cutter to cut out shapes.
Sprinkle cinnamon and sugar
over the tops; bake at 375°F
for 10-12 minutes, or until light
golden brown. This is useful if
you have scraps of dough left
after shaping your pie.

■ Decorate your pies using small
cookie cutters to cut shapes;
place them around the rim of your
pie or on top of the lattice.

Chocolate Chip
PEANUT PIE

Pareve | **Yield** 10-12 servings

Pecan pie is great, but why should the pecans have all the fun? If you're like me and always enjoy peanuts, this is the dessert for you! While first making this dessert, and every time I've made it since, I couldn't help but think, "This recipe is genius." I know it sounds a bit conceited, but when you make this, I know you'll feel the same way.

¾ **cup** dark corn syrup

¾ **cup** creamy peanut butter

¾ **cup** sugar

2 eggs

1 **teaspoon** vanilla extract

1 **cup** roasted salted peanuts, coarsely chopped

1 **cup** chocolate chips

1 ready-made graham cracker crust, preferably chocolate

chopped peanuts, chocolate sauce, and whipped cream, optional, for garnish

1. Preheat oven to 350°F.

2. In a small bowl, whisk together corn syrup, peanut butter, sugar, eggs, and vanilla until smooth.

3. Add peanuts and chocolate chips; stir until evenly distributed.

4. Pour mixture into graham cracker crust.

5. Bake for 45 minutes. Filling may be slightly soft in the center, but it will firm up as it cools.

6. Serve at room temperature. Garnish with chopped peanuts, chocolate sauce, and whipped cream, if desired.

Note You might think this would be even more delicious when served warm, but trust me — it's best served at room temperature, when you'll get the optimal texture and maximum flavor. This dessert is very rich, so don't be tempted to cut big slices.

Plan Ahead This pie freezes well in an airtight container.

HOT GOOEY
Caramel Pie

Dairy or **Pareve** | **Yield** 2 pies, each 8-10 servings

In the years that I've been developing and writing recipes, I've made a number that have been really popular, some of which you can find in this book. None, however, have been as iconic and popular as my Hot Gooey Caramel Pie. When trying to figure out why this recipe took off so well, I thought about how different this dessert is. While other recipes are exciting takes on familiar ideas and flavors, this one was so unusual and different that I didn't even know what I was making at first. It started with some ingredients in my pantry that I wanted to use up, and ended with a dessert that I could barely even name — but that everyone raved about. This pie has been made in numerous countries all over the world, graced many special-occasion tables, and enhanced many meals. And over and over again, fans have raved, "It's just SO good."

2 sticks (1 cup) butter or trans-fat-free margarine

8 oz cream cheese or soy cream cheese

1½ cups brown sugar

¼ cup light corn syrup

2 eggs

1 teaspoon baking soda

2 teaspoons vanilla extract

1½ cups flour

1 cup caramel chips

2 ready-made graham cracker pie crusts

vanilla ice cream, for serving, optional

Caramel Sauce (page 194) for serving, optional

1. Heat oven to 350°F.

2. In the bowl of an electric mixer, on medium speed, cream together butter and cream cheese until smooth. Add brown sugar and corn syrup; beat until smooth and creamy.

3. Add eggs, baking soda, and vanilla, beating to combine after each addition.

4. Reduce mixer speed to low; add flour. Beat until combined. Stir in caramel chips.

5. Divide batter between pie crusts. Bake for 30-35 minutes, until the center is just set (it will still be jiggly).

6. Serve warm with ice cream and caramel sauce (optional).

Note As the name suggests, the pie is gooey — and it doesn't cut into the neatest slices when warm. For a fancier presentation, make mini pies (see Variation) or serve it closer to room temperature, when it won't be as gooey.

Variation For neater serving, bake in mini graham cracker crusts or ramekins for 22-24 minutes.

Plan Ahead This pie freezes well in an airtight container. Defrost and reheat before serving.

Cookie Dough
FUDGE PIE

Dairy or **Pareve** | **Yield** 8-10 servings

This delicious pie, and its enormous popularity with thousands and thousands of readers, is the ultimate proof that there's a little kid inside us all, a kid who appreciates the simple pleasures of our childhood. Things like a rich, fudgy pie. Things like chocolate chip cookie dough and fudgy chocolate, straight from the mixer. This might not be the most sophisticated dessert, but it's a guaranteed crowd pleaser!

1 ready-made graham cracker pie crust

COOKIE DOUGH LAYER

2 **Tablespoons** oil

¼ **cup** brown sugar

2 **Tablespoons** sugar

½ **teaspoon** vanilla extract

1 **Tablespoon** milk or soy milk

½ **cup** flour

⅓ **cup** mini chocolate chips

FUDGE LAYER

1 **cup** oil

1 **cup** sugar

1 **teaspoon** vanilla extract

¼ **teaspoon** baking powder

2 **eggs**

½ **cup** flour

⅓ **cup** unsweetened cocoa powder

1. Preheat oven to 350°F.

2. **Prepare the cookie dough layer:** In the bowl of an electric mixer, on medium speed, beat together oil and sugars until combined.

3. Add vanilla, milk, and flour; beat until smooth. Add chocolate chips; stir to distribute evenly.

4. Remove cookie dough from mixer bowl to a second bowl; set aside. There is no need to wash the bowl before going on to the next step.

5. **Prepare the fudge layer:** In the bowl of an electric mixer, on medium speed, beat together oil and sugar until combined.

6. Add vanilla, baking powder, and eggs. Beat until smooth. Reduce mixer speed to low; add flour and cocoa. Beat until combined.

7. Pour the fudge layer into the graham cracker crust. Break off small pieces of the cookie dough and place evenly onto fudge layer to cover fudge. Push some pieces into the fudge so that they are buried or partially buried.

8. Bake for 40 minutes. Remove from oven; set aside to cool.

Note This pie is great at room temperature, warm, or even slightly frozen! Serve ice cream with a warm pie or whipped cream with a room temperature or cold pie.

Variation Instead of baking in a graham cracker crust, bake these in 6 individual ramekins. They'll only need about 25 minutes of baking time.

Plan Ahead This pie freezes well in an airtight container. If reheating it to serve warm, reheat uncovered.

A

B

C

D

E

QUICK AND EASY
Cherry Tarts

Pareve | **Yield** 25 small tarts

While I am generally not a fan of store-bought dough (especially because homemade pie crust is extremely easy to make!), it's sometimes nice to pull a package of frozen dough from the freezer and turn out a delicious homemade dessert a short while later. I make this filling even in the winter, using frozen cherries, and enjoy a taste of summer. While you technically can substitute canned cherry pie filling, this homemade filling is so easy to make, and it's immeasurably better than the canned version.

4 cups fresh cherries, pitted (see Note)

2 Tablespoons lemon juice

2 Tablespoons water

⅔ cup sugar

3 Tablespoons cornstarch

25 small (about 2½-inch) puff pastry squares

1. In a medium pot, over medium heat, combine cherries, lemon juice, water, and sugar. Sift cornstarch over mixture; stir to dissolve cornstarch.

2. Bring mixture to a boil, then lower heat; simmer for about ten minutes, until the liquid is thickened and starting to gel. Remove from heat; set aside to cool.

3. Preheat oven to 350°F. Line two baking sheets with parchment paper; set aside.

4. Working with one puff pastry square at a time, fold over about one-eighth inch on each side to form a small well. Press down well on each side to ensure it sticks. Spoon a small amount (4-6 cherries) of filling into the well. Place onto prepared baking sheet. Repeat with remaining dough and filling. Do not crowd the pan.

5. Bake for 30 minutes, until the edges are light golden brown.

Notes ■ These tarts are best served warm. I like to add a scoop of vanilla ice cream on top of each tart. ■ You can use frozen cherries instead of fresh; defrost first and drain off the liquid.

Variations ■ Make apple tarts using the same method, substituting the apple filling on page 120. ■ Make a traditional cherry pie with this filling in place of the one on page 116, following the rest of the instructions there.

Plan Ahead You can freeze these stored between layers of parchment paper so the filling doesn't stick to the other tarts.

Salted Chocolate Peanut Butter *TARTLETS*

Dairy or **Pareve** | **Yield** 6 tarts

The shortbread crust of these tartlets has a wonderful flavor and delicate texture. Baking them empty means that you can fill these tarts with anything you like! I've made them for a party and offered the guests their choice of chocolate filled, as you see here, or fruit and cream filled, for a lighter variety (see Variation). These tarts are considered individually sized, but they are fairly rich, so you may want to cut them in half when plating.

SHORTBREAD CRUST

2 sticks (1 cup) butter or trans-fat-free margarine

1 teaspoon kosher salt

1 teaspoon vanilla extract

½ cup powdered sugar

2 cups flour

PEANUT BUTTER FILLING

6 Tablespoons (¼ cup + 2 Tablespoons) creamy peanut butter

6 Tablespoons (¼ cup + 2 Tablespoons) powdered sugar

½ stick (¼ cup) butter or trans-fat-free margarine

CHOCOLATE FILLING

18 oz semisweet dark chocolate, cut into chunks

1 cup heavy whipping cream or nondairy whip topping

coarse sea salt, for sprinkling, optional, but highly recommended

1. Prepare the crust: Preheat oven to 350°F.

2. In the bowl of an electric mixer, on medium speed, beat together butter, salt, vanilla, and sugar until smooth.

3. Reduce mixer speed to low. Add flour; beat until it just comes together to a dough. Do not overmix; the dough may be slightly crumbly.

4. Divide dough into 6 equal parts. Press each portion of dough into the bottom and sides of a mini (4-5-inch) tart pan.

5. Bake tart shells for about 18 minutes, until light golden brown and somewhat firm. As soon as shells come out of the oven, use a heatproof utensil or cup to press down along the bottom and edges to reinforce the shape. Set aside to cool completely before filling.

6. Prepare the peanut butter filling: Combine all ingredients in a small bowl; stir until smooth. Spread a very thin layer of mixture into each tart shell.

7. Prepare the chocolate filling: Place chocolate chunks into a medium heatproof bowl.

8. In a small pot, cook cream over medium heat until it just reaches a boil. Pour hot cream over chocolate; whisk quickly to melt chocolate. If the cream cools too much before chocolate is completely melted, place the bowl over a small pot of boiling water and whisk until all the chunks have melted.

9. Pour chocolate filling into tart shells until almost full. Don't fill them all the way to the top or the filling may spill over the edges and they won't be as pretty.

10. Sprinkle sea salt over tart, if desired; set aside to cool completely until firm.

Note Use various shapes and sizes of tart pans; make sure to adjust baking time accordingly. The shell should not exceed a half-inch in height.

Variation Instead of chocolate tarts, fill these with the Mini Pavlova cream (page 150) and top with fruit of your choice.

Plan Ahead Freeze completed tarts in an airtight container. For best results, freeze empty shells; fill just before serving.

■ Plating the perfect dessert is not just about taste. Make sure to think about the color, the texture, the dish your dessert is served on, and the art behind the arrangement. And most of all, they should all work together. Don't stick on garnishes that won't taste good with your dessert, simply because they will look pretty. Compose the plate as if it were a painting and you are the artist.

■ Don't skip the drama element! Artfully plated sauces, layers and height, cool garnishes (such as a shard of bark; pages 160-161) all add an element of drama to the plate, which in turn ensures that you'll impress your guests.

■ Vary the size of your dessert depending on its purpose. For example, serve mousse in a 1-2-ounce cup for a sweet table or kiddush, or in a 4-6-ounce cup to end a formal meal.

DESSERTS *AND* PARTY TREATS

- Texture is an important part of a dessert presentation. If serving a soft dessert (such as a mousse or sorbet), think about adding a crunchy element, such as Edible Dessert Cups (page 138) or Chocolate Crumbs (page 128). When serving a dessert such as a pie, consider adding a scoop of ice cream for textural contrast.

- Think about the dessert as a whole: When serving a heavy dessert (such as Cookie Dough Fudge Pie (page 112) or Salted Chocolate Peanut Butter Tartlets (page 124), consider adding fresh fruit, such as citrus supremes or berries, to the plate, to give it a lighter feel.

- For tips on setting up a dessert table at a party, see page 202.

Neapolitan
TRIFLES

Dairy or **Pareve** | **Yield** 12-14 (6-oz) trifles

This recipe was created out of necessity. I needed a dessert recipe that looked pretty, traveled well. and could be made ahead and frozen when fully completed. This one fits all of those criteria. It freezes well, can be stored frozen and transported in a sealed jar, looks gorgeous, and tastes great. It was a hit, and surely will be a hit at your parties too!

CHOCOLATE CRUMBS

1 cup flour

½ cup unsweetened cocoa powder

⅔ cup brown sugar

⅓ cup oil

STRAWBERRY MOUSSE

1 cup heavy whipping cream or nondairy whip topping

1 cup strawberry pie filling, puréed

8 oz cream cheese or soy cream cheese

⅓ cup sour cream or soy sour cream

1 teaspoon vanilla extract

1 cup powdered sugar

VANILLA CREAM

1 cup heavy whipping cream or nondairy whip topping

⅓ cup powdered sugar

1. **Prepare the chocolate crumbs:** Preheat oven to 375°F. Line a baking sheet with parchment paper; set aside.

2. Combine all crumb ingredients in a bowl. Mix until combined and the texture of coarse crumbs. (I found it easiest to mix this with my fingers.)

3. Spread the crumbs in a single layer on prepared baking sheet; bake for 8 minutes. Remove from oven; cool completely before assembling the trifles.

4. **Prepare the strawberry mousse:** In the bowl of an electric mixer fitted with the whisk attachment, on high speed, beat whipping cream until stiff peaks form. Remove whipped cream to another bowl. There's no need to wash the bowl before continuing.

5. Add pie filling, cream cheese, sour cream, and vanilla to mixer bowl. Beat on medium speed until combined and smooth. Add powdered sugar; beat until incorporated.

6. Using a rubber spatula, gently fold whipped cream into strawberry mixture until combined. Set aside.

7. **Prepare the vanilla cream:** In the bowl of an electric mixer fitted with the whisk attachment, on high speed, beat whipping cream until stiff peaks form. Reduce mixer speed to low. Gradually beat in powdered sugar until combined.

8. **Assembly:** Place crumbs into a 6-ounce jar or cup, filling it about one-quarter full. Spoon or pipe strawberry mousse over crumbs, filling container a little more than three-quarters full. Pipe on vanilla cream, filling container almost to the top. Repeat with remaining jars.

Note Use canned pie filling, or use the filling for *Strawberry Rhubarb Hand Pies* (p. 118), using additional strawberries to replace the rhubarb.

Variation Substitute a container of strawberry ice cream for the mousse to create an ice cream trifle.

Plan Ahead These trifles freeze beautifully (see introduction)! Move them into the fridge for a couple of hours before serving to allow them to soften a bit.

Egg-Free Chocolate
MOUSSE

Dairy or **Pareve** | **Yield** 12-15 servings

Chocolate Mousse is one of those basic recipes that we all need to have up our sleeves. When creating a great recipe to share in this book, I listened to my readers' frequent request: They want an egg-free chocolate mousse. Well, here you go — no eggs, but still delicious!

1 cup heavy whipping cream or nondairy whip topping

8 oz semisweet chocolate, melted and cooled

1 teaspoon instant coffee dissolved in 1 Tablespoon boiling water

2 Tablespoons amaretto or coffee liqueur

1 cup powdered sugar

whipped cream and chocolate shavings, optional, for garnish

1. In the bowl of an electric mixer fitted with the whisk attachment, on high speed, beat whipping cream until stiff peaks form. Set aside.

2. In a small bowl, whisk together melted chocolate, coffee, and liqueur until smooth. Add powdered sugar; stir until combined.

3. Pour chocolate mixture into whipped cream. Beat lightly until mostly combined, then switch to a rubber spatula to fully incorporate.

4. Spoon or pipe mousse into small cups. If desired, top with additional whipped cream and chocolate shavings.

Note This is a light and fluffy mousse. If you prefer a dark and rich chocolate mousse, opt for the chocolate layer of the Chocolate Peppermint Mousse Trifles (page 136).

Plan Ahead Mousse freezes well in an airtight container. If you plan to serve these in individual portions, it's best to freeze it in individual jars or containers, so it defrosts and serves nicely.

Lemon Cheesecake
MOUSSE CUPS

Dairy or **Pareve** | **Yield** about 20 (2-oz) servings

It's a known truth that the good deeds you do come back to help you out in life. In the case of this dessert, I offered to help my sister-in-law Freidi by making dessert for a party she was hosting. I came up with these gorgeous — and delicious — mousse cups. The resulting treat was amazing, but the real payback for helping her came when this recipe went viral. There's no better feeling than when I know that people are making my recipes, and in this case, there were tens of thousands of people, all raving about the incredible taste, the light texture, and the guaranteed-to-please qualities of this recipe.

LEMON MOUSSE

1 cup heavy whipping cream or nondairy whip topping

1 cup canned lemon pie filling

12 oz cream cheese or soy cream cheese

1 teaspoon vanilla extract

few drops yellow food coloring, optional

1 cup powdered sugar

GRAHAM CRACKER CRUMBLE

½ cup graham cracker crumbs

2 Tablespoons sugar

2 Tablespoons oil or melted butter

1. In the bowl of an electric mixer, on high speed, whip cream until stiff.

2. Remove whipped cream from mixer; set aside. (No need to wash the bowl before continuing.) Add lemon pie filling and cream cheese to the mixer bowl; beat on medium speed until smooth.

3. Add vanilla, food coloring (if using), and powdered sugar; beat until combined.

4. Using a rubber spatula, gradually (in two or three batches) fold whipped cream into the cream cheese mixture, until it is fully incorporated. Set aside.

5. **Prepare the graham cracker crumble:** Combine graham cracker crumbs, sugar, and oil in a small bowl until stiff crumbs form.

6. **Assembly:** Place a small amount of crumble into a small (about 2-ounce) cup. Pipe mousse over the crumbs to almost fill the cup; add more crumbs on top. Serve chilled.

Notes ■ Instead of small cups, use 4-6-ounce cups or jars. ■ Replace this Crumble with crumbled cake, such as Triple Citrus Bundt Cake (page 66) or Ultimate Vanilla Bundt Cake (page 65).

Variation In place of lemon pie filling, use pie filling flavor of your choice. Make sure to blend it well, so it's smooth and creamy (like the lemon pie filling) before using.

Plan Ahead These freeze well in an airtight container. Prepare completely, cover well, and freeze. Defrost in the refrigerator for an hour or so. They're great partially frozen, too.

Praline Mousse
CANNOLI

Dairy or **Pareve** | **Yield** 45 cannoli

If you've never experienced praline, it's a fantastic flavor that you'll want to try. Praline paste, made from a combination of ground nuts — usually hazelnuts — and sugar, is available in the baking aisle of many grocery stores. The praline flavor in this mousse is distinct and delicious, and it presents nicely in these cannoli shells.

1 cup heavy whipping cream or nondairy whip topping

12 oz cream cheese or soy cream cheese

½ cup praline paste

1½ teaspoons vanilla extract

1½ cups powdered sugar

45 fillable cannoli (wafer roll) shells

1   In the bowl of an electric mixer fitted with a whisk attachment, on high speed, beat cream until stiff peaks form. Remove to another bowl and set aside. (There is no need to wash the mixer bowl before continuing.)

2   Add cream cheese, praline paste, and vanilla to the mixer bowl; beat on medium-high speed until combined and smooth. Add powdered sugar; beat until smooth.

3   Using a rubber spatula, gently fold half the whipped cream into praline mixture. Stir until incorporated. Add remaining whipped cream; fold in gently until incorporated. Do not overmix.

4   Refrigerate mixture for about an hour until firm enough to pipe. Transfer to a piping bag fitted with a large round or star tip. Insert the tip halfway into the shell and pipe in the filling, withdrawing the tip as you go. Turn the cannoli shell around and pipe into the other end until it is full. Repeat with remaining shells and mousse.

5   Place cannoli on a tray in the fridge or freezer until ready to serve.

Note Some people enjoy these most when the cannoli are frozen. I think they're best when partially frozen, so for best results, freeze the cannoli and take them out about an hour before serving.

Variations ■ Pipe the mousse into a glass and layer with cake or cookie crumbs, or use the crumbs from the Neapolitan Trifles (page 128). ■ Fill cannoli shell with another mousse in this chapter, including Strawberry Mousse (page 128), Chocolate Mousse (page 136), Lemon Mousse (page 132) or Peppermint Mousse (page 136).

Plan Ahead These freeze well in an airtight container or tray. For best results, freeze them with plenty of space between them on the tray, so the piping isn't disturbed. Be careful not to place anything heavy on top of the container, as cannoli shells are delicate and easily crushed.

Chocolate Peppermint
MOUSSE TRIFLES

Dairy or **Pareve** | **Yield** 20-24 servings

I firmly believe that food has to look great in addition to having great flavor. Luckily, this treat shines in the taste and looks department! The layers of brown and pink look so pretty together and the crushed candies on the top really add to the "wow" factor, making these perfect to serve at your next party.

PEPPERMINT MOUSSE

1 cup heavy whipping cream or nondairy whip topping

1 stick (½ cup) butter or trans-fat-free margarine

8 oz cream cheese or soy cream cheese

1 teaspoon vanilla extract

½ teaspoon mint extract

1 cup powdered sugar

1 cup crushed peppermint candies

CHOCOLATE MOUSSE

1 cup heavy whipping cream or nondairy whip topping

8 oz cream cheese or soy cream cheese

1 cup chocolate-hazelnut spread

1 teaspoon vanilla extract

crushed peppermint candies, optional

1. **Prepare the peppermint mousse:** In the bowl of an electric mixer fitted with the whisk attachment, on high speed, whip cream until stiff. Remove to another bowl; set aside. (No need to wash the mixer bowl before continuing.)

2. Reduce mixer speed to medium; add butter, cream cheese, vanilla, and mint extract; beat until smooth. Add powdered sugar; beat until combined.

3. Using a rubber spatula, gently (in two or three batches), fold whipped cream into cream cheese mixture until fully incorporated. Gently fold in crushed candies until evenly distributed and mousse is pink. Place in the fridge to chill while you prepare the chocolate mousse.

4. **Prepare the chocolate mousse:** In the bowl of an electric mixer fitted with the whisk attachment, on high speed, whip cream until stiff. Remove to another bowl; set aside. (No need to wash the mixer bowl before continuing.)

5. Reduce mixer speed to medium. Add cream cheese, chocolate-hazelnut spread, and vanilla to the mixer bowl; beat until smooth.

6. Using a rubber spatula, gently (in two or three batches), fold whipped cream into cream cheese mixture until fully incorporated. Set aside.

7. **Assemble:** Pipe alternating layers of peppermint and chocolate mousse into a small cup. For the best effect, use a tall 2-oz shot glass. Top with crushed peppermint candies, optional. Repeat with remaining mousse.

Variations ■ Omit chocolate mousse; layer mousse with Chocolate Crumbs (page 128). ■ Substitute Strawberry Mousse (page 128) for Peppermint Mousse.

Plan Ahead Trifles freeze well in an airtight container. Defrost for an hour or two before serving (they're great while still partially frozen).

EDIBLE
Cookie Cups

Pareve | **Yield** 15 large cups

If you're planning a party and looking for an elegant dessert, here's a fun — and delicious — way to dress up something as simple as ice cream, sorbet, or mousse: edible cups. These cups are made of tuile cookies, traditional French cookies that are wafer thin and flexible when they comes out of the oven, allowing you to shape them as you like.

½ cup oil

1½ teaspoons vanilla extract

1 Tablespoon light corn syrup or honey

4 egg whites

¾ cup sugar

1⅛ cups (1 cup plus 2 Tablespoons) flour

1. Preheat oven to 350°F. Line 2 baking sheets with parchment paper; set aside.

2. In a small bowl, whisk together oil, vanilla, corn syrup, and egg whites until combined. Add sugar and flour; whisk until smooth and thick. The mixture should have the texture of thick paste.

3. Spread about a heaping tablespoon of the paste in a circle about 5 inches in diameter onto the prepared baking sheets. Spread the paste as thin as possible without causing any holes in the circle. Spread two circles per baking sheet.

4. Bake for 5-6 minutes, until the edges start to turn golden.

5. Drape the tuile over the bottom of a small (about 4 ounce) cup, jar, or half-cup measuring cup. Leave in place until firm, about a minute.

6. You have only a few seconds to work while the tuiles are pliable enough to shape. If they cool down before you shape them, place them into the hot oven for about 30 seconds and they will become pliable again. Repeat with remaining paste, baking no more than 2-4 tuiles at a time so you have time to shape them before they set.

Note For the neatest cookie, it's best to trace two circles on the back of the parchment paper before lining the pan. Use the circle as a guide when spreading the paste.

Variation Instead of forming cups with the tuiles, bake smaller circles, then drape each cookie over the side of a glass for the traditional curved shape, or curl it around the handle of a wooden spoon for a cigar shape.

Plan Ahead Store at room temperature in an airtight container for a few days, or freeze. Handle with care to ensure they don't break while being stored. Exposure to air will cause them to soften and lose their shape.

Pretzel-Crusted Peanut Butter
CHEESECAKE

Dairy or **Pareve** | **Yield** 12-14 servings

Pretzels. Peanut butter. Chocolate. This dessert is for all the people out there who crave that sweet and salty combo — this cheesecake has it all!

CRUST

2 cups coarse pretzel crumbs

¼ cup brown sugar

1½ sticks (¾ cup) butter or trans-fat-free margarine, melted

FILLING

3 (8-oz) packages cream cheese or soy cream cheese

¾ cup sour cream or soy sour cream

¾ cup creamy peanut butter

1 cup sugar

1 teaspoon vanilla extract

3 eggs

FUDGE TOPPING

½ cup heavy whipping cream or nondairy whip topping

6 ounces good-quality semisweet dark chocolate, chopped

1. Preheat oven to 350°F.

2. Prepare the crust: Combine pretzel crumbs, sugar, and butter in a small bowl. Mix until combined; the mixture should have a slightly wet and sticky texture.

3. Press crumbs onto the bottom and up the sides of a 9-inch springform pan. Smooth sides of crust by pressing the side of a round cup, such as a measuring cup, against the edge. Wrap the bottom of the pan in foil to prevent leakage while baking. Place pan in the freezer to become firm while you prepare the filling.

4. Prepare the filling: In the bowl of an electric mixer, on medium speed, beat together cream cheese, sour cream, and peanut butter until creamy.

5. Add sugar, vanilla, and eggs. Beat until combined. Don't overmix.

6. Pour batter into prepared crust. Bake for 55-60 minutes, until the edges are set and the center is slightly soft. Do not overbake. Set cheesecake aside to cool completely before adding the topping.

7. Prepare the fudge topping: Heat cream in a small pot until it just comes to a boil. Place chopped chocolate into a heatproof bowl; pour hot cream over it. Whisk until chocolate melts and mixture is smooth. Let cool for 2-3 minutes, until slightly thickened, then pour over cooled cheesecake. Refrigerate until topping is set. Store in refrigerator.

Variation Use graham cracker crust (page 142) in place of pretzel crust.

Plan Ahead This cheesecake freezes well in an airtight container. Defrost completely before serving.

Neapolitan Zebra
CHEESECAKE

Dairy or **Pareve** | **Yield** 12-14 servings

It's a well-known adage that people eat with their eyes first, and you won't find a more impressive, gorgeous dessert to amaze your guests than this one. While it's somewhat intimidating to make all the layers and then scoop them out carefully, the incredible result will be well worth it — not to mention the delightful Neapolitan flavor combination that we all know and love.

CRUST

1½ **cups** graham cracker crumbs

¼ **cup** sugar

6 **Tablespoons** butter or trans-fat-free margarine, melted

CHOCOLATE LAYER

8 **oz** cream cheese or soy cream cheese

½ **cup** sour cream or soy sour cream

½ **cup** sugar

2 eggs

1 **teaspoon** vanilla extract

¼ **cup** milk or soy milk

¼ **cup** unsweetened cocoa powder

¼ **cup** flour

(continues on facing page)

1. **Prepare the crust:** Mix crust ingredients together until combined and mixture is the texture of wet sand. Press mixture along the bottom and up the sides of a 9-inch springform pan; press on the sides to smooth the crust. Place crust into the freezer while you prepare the batter.

2. **Prepare the batter:** Place ingredients for strawberry layer, chocolate layer, and vanilla layer into separate bowls. Using an electric mixer or a whisk, whisk ingredients in each bowl until smooth.

3. Preheat oven to 350°F.

4. **Assembly:** Remove the crust from the freezer. [A] Using a small cup or squeeze bottle, place about ¼ cup of chocolate batter in the center of the crust. [B] Next, place a scoop of vanilla batter in the center of the chocolate. This will cause the chocolate batter to spread out toward the edge. [C] Then, place a scoop of strawberry batter in the center of the vanilla, causing the previous layers to spread out toward the edge of the pan as well. [D] As you add layers, the pan will fill up and you'll see the zebra effect starting to take shape. [E] Repeat with the remaining batter, alternating the flavors.

5. Bake for 65 minutes. To prevent the top from cracking, turn off heat and leave cheesecake in the oven to cool slowly for at least an hour before placing in fridge.

Note To make strawberry purée: Completely defrost frozen strawberries; purée in food processor until smooth. 1 cup whole strawberries = about ½ cup purée.

Variation Divide batter between two store-bought graham cracker crusts. Bake for 40-45 minutes.

Plan Ahead This cheesecake freezes well when wrapped airtight. Leave it in the fridge to defrost completely before serving.

VANILLA LAYER

8 oz cream cheese or soy cream cheese

½ cup sour cream or soy sour cream

2 eggs

½ cup sugar

2 teaspoons vanilla extract

¼ cup milk or soy milk

6 Tablespoons flour

STRAWBERRY LAYER

8 oz cream cheese or soy cream cheese

½ cup sour cream or soy sour cream

½ cup sugar

2 eggs

¼ cup flour

½ cup strawberry purée (see Note)

1 teaspoon strawberry extract (optional, but strongly recommended)

several drops red food coloring (optional but recommended)

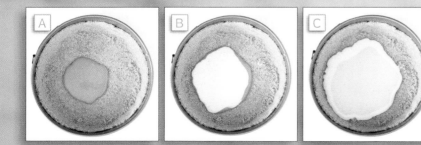
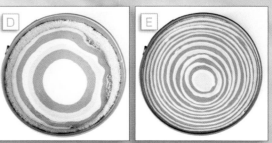

Confetti Cheesecake
CUPCAKES

Dairy or **Pareve** | **Yield** 9-10 servings

These adorable little cheesecakes make a great party treat. They're kid-friendly thanks to the color, and adult-friendly thanks to the great flavor! Bonus: They're really easy to make!

9-10 vanilla sandwich cookies

8 oz cream cheese or soy cream cheese

⅓ cup sugar

2 eggs

1 teaspoon vanilla extract

⅓ cup colorful sprinkles

TOPPING

½ cup heavy whipping cream or nondairy whip topping

¼ cup powdered sugar

sprinkles, optional, for decorating

1. Preheat oven to 350°F. Line a cupcake pan with paper liners. (You will only need 9-10.) Place a sandwich cookie into each liner.

2. In a small bowl, whisk together cream cheese, sugar, eggs, and vanilla until smooth. Add sprinkles; stir gently to distribute evenly.

3. Divide filling between prepared liners. Bake for 17-18 minutes, or until tops are set. Set aside to cool completely.

4. **Prepare the topping:** Whip cream until stiff peaks form. Stir in powdered sugar. Place topping into a piping bag; pipe over cooled cheesecakes.

5. Decorate with remaining sprinkles.

Variation For cookies 'n cream cheesecake cupcakes: Substitute chocolate sandwich cookies for the vanilla cookie base. Substitute ⅓ cup chocolate sandwich cookie crumbs for the sprinkles.

Plan Ahead These mini cheesecakes freeze well in an airtight container or zip-lock bag. For best results, freeze them without the whipped cream topping; add it just before serving.

Healthy Summer
FRUIT CRUMBLES

Pareve | **Yield** 6-8 servings

One of the great things about summer (aside from the sunshine, long days, and glorious weather) is the plethora of juicy, sweet fruits. Bite into one, and the juice dribbles down your chin … but you don't care about the mess because it's just that delicious. Because these fruits are so great on their own, there's no need to do much to them — so I kept these crumbles really simple.

3 small peaches, peeled

3 plums

1 cup blueberries

1½ cups cherries, pitted and quartered

2 Tablespoons oil

⅓ cup sugar or dry sweetener, such as Splenda

2 teaspoons cinnamon

CRUMBLE

2 cups old-fashioned rolled oats

1 cup flour (white whole wheat is best)

¾ cup chopped pecans, walnuts, or almonds

¾ cup sugar or dry sweetener, such as Splenda

¼ cup oil

2 Tablespoons unsweetened applesauce (or additional oil)

2 egg whites

1. Preheat oven to 350°F.

2. Cut peaches and plums into small chunks. In a medium bowl, combine fruit, oil, sugar, and cinnamon. Toss to coat all fruit evenly. Divide mixture among 6-8 ramekins, leaving room for the topping.

3. Prepare the crumble: Combine oats, flour, nuts, and sugar. Add oil, applesauce, and egg whites; mix to form coarse crumbs.

4. Divide crumbs among the filled ramekins. Place ramekins on baking sheet; bake for 30-35 minutes, until the fruit is soft and the topping is crunchy. For best results, serve warm.

Note Place any extra crumble on a baking sheet; bake along with the crumbles. Use to top yogurt and ice cream, or just enjoy it as a granola-type snack.

Variation The recipe serves as a guide, but you can change the fruit mixture based on your personal preference and what's available.

Plan Ahead Freeze in airtight containers. For best results, reheat at 350°F, uncovered, before serving.

Chocolate
CREPES

Dairy or **Pareve** | **Yield** 10 servings

Crepes are one of those desserts that seem complicated and difficult to pull off, but they're actually really simple to make! The trick is to work with a good nonstick pan, let your pan get hot enough before you start, and not to attempt to flip the crepe too soon. A crepe pan is an inexpensive and worthwhile investment, as crepes are an easy and delicious treat.

3 eggs

2 egg yolks

1 cup milk or soy milk

⅔ cup flour

⅓ cup unsweetened cocoa powder

⅓ cup sugar

choice of fillings (see below)

1. Whisk all ingredients in a small bowl until completely smooth. For best results, place the batter in the refrigerator for an hour or two, or up to overnight.

2. Heat a nonstick crepe pan or frying pan over medium heat. Spray with nonstick cooking spray.

3. When pan is hot, pour a quarter-cup of batter onto the pan; immediately tilt the pan to spread the batter over the pan's entire surface. Crepe should be very thin. Fry for about 1 minute, until the crepe has set, then flip it over and fry for about 30 seconds to a minute on the other side. Don't flip your crepe too soon; the batter should appear cooked, and just slightly wet before you flip it. Remove from heat and set aside. Repeat with remaining batter.

4. To serve, fill crepe with your choice of fillings, then roll or fold in half, top as you like, and enjoy.

Filling Options

Spreads: Jam, chocolate spread, marshmallow fluff, peanut butter

Flavored Whipped Cream: Combine 1 cup whipped cream with 1 cup fruit preserves, OR ½ cup of chocolate spread.

Fruit: Sliced bannanas, sliced strawberries, fresh berries

Topping Options

Chocolate Sauce, Caramel Sauce, Strawberry Sauce (all on page 195), powdered sugar, whipped cream, ice cream, chopped nuts, cookie crumbs, crushed graham crackers, sprinkles

Note I like to serve these on a "crepe bar" for a fun party treat. Prepare crepes, bowls of fillings and toppings, and let your guests create their own

Plan Ahead While crepes are delicious when enjoyed fresh, you can make them ahead and freeze them flat between layers of parchment

Mini Fruit-Filled
PAVLOVAS

Dairy or **Pareve** | **Yield** 12-15 servings

These light and airy treats make a phenomenal (and not too heavy) ending to a special-occasion meal. And because they look fancy but aren't too difficult to make, they are ideal for serving at a party or on a dessert table.

4 egg whites

1¼ cups sugar

2 teaspoons cornstarch

½ teaspoon vanilla extract

1 teaspoon lemon juice

FILLING

1 cup heavy whipping cream or nondairy whip topping

8 oz cream cheese or soy cream cheese

1 teaspoon vanilla extract

⅓ cup powdered sugar

approximately 3 cups seasonal fruit, cut into small pieces

1. Preheat oven to 250°F. Line a baking sheet with parchment paper; set aside.

2. In the bowl of an electric mixer fitted with the whisk attachment, on high speed, beat egg whites until soft peaks form (whites should be thick but not stiff or holding their shape). Add half the sugar, then continue to beat until stiff peaks form (whites hold their shape when touched). Add remaining sugar; continue to beat until sugar is incorporated and whites are shiny and stiff, about a minute or two.

3. Sift the cornstarch over the whites; add vanilla and lemon juice. Use a rubber spatula to gently fold in the additions.

4. Spoon whites onto prepared baking sheet to form mounds, 2½-3 inches in diameter; press down in the center to form a well deep enough to hold the filling. For neatest, most consistent results, trace circles on the underside of the parchment paper; use them as your guide when forming the pavlovas.

5. Bake for 30 minutes; then turn the oven off, leaving the pavlovas inside to cool for an hour before removing them from the oven.

6. **Prepare the filling:** In the bowl of an electric mixer fitted with the whisk attachment, on high speed, beat cream until stiff.

7. Reduce mixer speed to medium; add cream cheese, vanilla, and sugar. Beat until smooth. Spoon filling into the well of each pavlova; top with fruit.

Variation For a more traditional whipped cream filling, omit the cream cheese from the filling. This variation is best with dairy cream, as nondairy whip topping is best with additional flavoring.

Plan ahead You can make the pavlova shells up to a week ahead of time and store them in an airtight container at room temperature. Fill them just before serving.

Cookies 'n Cream
STUFFED WAFFLES

Dairy or **Pareve** | **Yield** 8 servings

Nowadays, everyone loves to have "breakfast for dinner," but why not take it a step further and have breakfast for dessert? In this indulgent recipe, I took a breakfast staple over the top with a delicious filling. Have fun topping these waffles with ice cream, whipped cream, sauces, or any other toppings to create the ultimate waffle sundae.

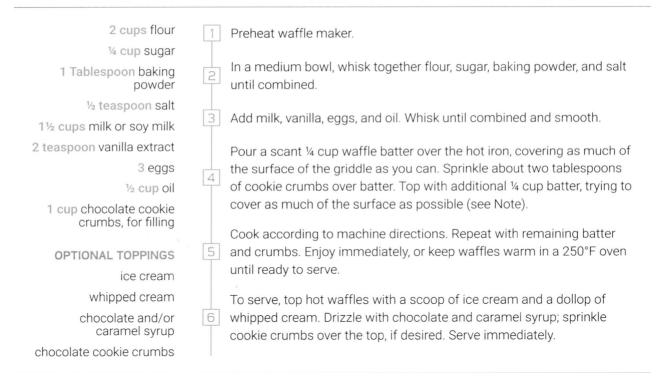

2 cups flour

¼ cup sugar

1 Tablespoon baking powder

½ teaspoon salt

1½ cups milk or soy milk

2 teaspoon vanilla extract

3 eggs

½ cup oil

1 cup chocolate cookie crumbs, for filling

OPTIONAL TOPPINGS

ice cream

whipped cream

chocolate and/or caramel syrup

chocolate cookie crumbs

1. Preheat waffle maker.

2. In a medium bowl, whisk together flour, sugar, baking powder, and salt until combined.

3. Add milk, vanilla, eggs, and oil. Whisk until combined and smooth.

4. Pour a scant ¼ cup waffle batter over the hot iron, covering as much of the surface of the griddle as you can. Sprinkle about two tablespoons of cookie crumbs over batter. Top with additional ¼ cup batter, trying to cover as much of the surface as possible (see Note).

5. Cook according to machine directions. Repeat with remaining batter and crumbs. Enjoy immediately, or keep waffles warm in a 250°F oven until ready to serve.

6. To serve, top hot waffles with a scoop of ice cream and a dollop of whipped cream. Drizzle with chocolate and caramel syrup; sprinkle cookie crumbs over the top, if desired. Serve immediately.

Note Different waffle makers will need different amounts of batter to fill the iron. The amount indicated here works to make round waffles, about 7 inches in diameter. If your waffle iron is a different size, consult the manual to see how much batter you'll need. Following the instructions above, add only half the usual amount of batter when first filling the waffle maker so that there will be room for the cookie crumbs; then add crumbs and pour on the remaining half of the batter.

Variations ■ For plain waffles, omit the cookie crumbs. ■ For an easier variation, fold the cookie crumbs into the batter. The effect won't be quite the same, but the flavor will still be great.

Plan Ahead Waffles freeze well in an airtight container. To reheat, defrost completely, then reheat on a baking sheet, in a single layer, at 250°F, until heated through.

Pecan Pie
CIGARS

Pareve | **Yield** 12-14 servings

Pecan pie is a comforting, classic American dessert. In this updated take, you will enjoy that sticky pie filling in a modern and beautiful presentation. You can present them as a restaurant-worthy dessert, as pictured, or simply serve them on a plate. Either way, you'll love the crisp exterior and the sticky interior of these great treats.

1 egg

½ cup sugar

⅔ cup dark corn syrup

1 Tablespoon oil

1 teaspoon vanilla extract

2 cups chopped pecans

12-14 (12 x 17-inch) phyllo sheets

1 egg, lightly beaten, for brushing

1. Preheat oven to 350°F. Line a baking sheet with parchment paper; set aside.

2. In a medium bowl, whisk together egg, sugar, corn syrup, oil, and vanilla until smooth. Add the pecans; switch from the whisk to a sturdy spoon. Stir until incorporated. The mixture will be very thick.

3. Work with one phyllo sheet at a time, keeping the rest covered with plastic wrap to prevent them from drying out. Fold a phyllo sheet in half to create a smaller rectangle, about 12 inches by 8.5 inches. Spread about two tablespoons of filling in a narrow line (about 6 inches in length) along the center of the rectangle. Leave plenty of space on each of the four sides for folding over the filling.

4. Starting with the shorter sides, fold each side over the filling; the ends should meet or almost meet in the center. Next, fold one of the longer sides over the filling. Roll rectangle along the length to form a cigar. Brush a bit of egg along the seam to seal it; then place cigar on prepared baking sheet.

5. Repeat with remaining phyllo and filling. Leave space between the cigars on the baking sheet, as some of the filling leaks out during baking. Brush egg onto each cigar.

6. Bake for about 18 minutes, until cigars are golden brown and crispy. Serve hot.

Note To plate as in the photo: Cut the cigars on the diagonal into varying lengths. Stand them up on a plate. Drizzle with Caramel Sauce (page 194); top with vanilla ice cream and salted pecans.

Plan Ahead Freeze cigars in an airtight container, between layers of parchment to avoid sticking. To reheat, defrost cigars; bake uncovered, in a single layer, at 350°F, for just a couple of minutes, until warmed through.

■ A candy thermometer is a special tool used in candy making, in order to get the sugar to a precise temperature. Sugar develops different textures at different temperatures, so this tool is needed to ensure the final product will have the correct texture. In this book, I only use a candy thermometer in one recipe, but in general, when you see it called for, don't be tempted to try the recipe without it.

■ When preparing treats for a party or event with a color scheme, you might want to dip candy and chocolate (such as truffles) into colored candy melts instead of chocolate. However, where chocolate tastes great, candy melts generally don't. Instead, therefore, I like to dip items into good quality chocolate, then drizzle colorful candy melts as an accent.

■ Give store-bought lollipops an adorable and homemade-looking spin: Apply a bit of corn syrup to the surface of the lollipop (this is best done using a food-safe paintbrush for the entire surface or a toothpick for tiny areas). Immediately sprinkle on sanding sugar, sugar pearls, or colored sprinkles, using the corn syrup as a "glue" to adhere the decorations. Set lollipops aside to dry and allow the decorations to set.

CANDY *AND* CHOCOLATE

■ When dipping Truffles (pages 158, 162) or other items in melted chocolate, dip the truffle ball into the melted chocolate using a dipping tool (available for a few dollars at craft or baking supply stores) or a large fork. Suspend the tool over the bowl of chocolate and gently tap to help all the excess chocolate drip off before placing the truffle onto parchment paper. This will ensure even, smooth coating and prevent a large "foot" of chocolate from gathering on the base.

■ Create decorative marshmallows for a fun party treat by pushing a lollipop stick halfway into the marshmallow, then dipping it into chocolate or candy melts. You can also decorate them with colored sanding sugar: Dip the marshmallow lightly into water, tapping off the excess water onto a napkin or paper towel, leaving a slightly damp marshmallow. Immediately roll it in colored sugar, then set aside to dry.

Chocolate
TRUFFLES

Dairy or **Pareve** | **Yield** 2½ dozen

There are a number of ways to make truffles, but only one way to make them indulgent, rich, and intense chocolate perfection. These truffles are delicious made with nondairy cream, but try them with real heavy cream and coated in milk chocolate for a truly memorable treat.

16 oz semisweet dark chocolate, chopped into very small chunks

1 cup heavy whipping cream or nondairy whip topping

1 teaspoon instant coffee dissolved in **1 Tablespoon** boiling water

10 ounces semisweet or milk chocolate, melted, for coating (see Note)

1. Place chocolate chunks into a medium heatproof bowl; set aside.

2. In a small pot, heat cream over medium heat until the edges start to bubble and it just comes to a boil. Do not overheat.

3. Pour hot cream over chocolate chunks and quickly stir, letting the heat of the cream melt the chocolate. It is easiest to do this using a whisk. Once chocolate has melted, the mixture should have a thick, fudgy texture (see Notes). Add coffee; stir until smooth.

4. Place bowl in the refrigerator for an hour or two, until chocolate mixture has thickened enough to roll into balls.

5. Use a small cookie scoop or heaping teaspoon to spoon out chocolate; roll the scoops into balls. Place chocolate balls onto a tray in the refrigerator to become firm.

6. Dip each chocolate ball into melted chocolate; roll it until fully coated, allowing excess chocolate to drip back into the bowl. Place truffles on parchment paper and place into refrigerator until chocolate coating has hardened. Store in fridge until ready to serve.

Notes ■ If the cream is hot and you work quickly, all the chocolate should melt. However, if the mixture cools and there are still lumps of unmelted chocolate, place the bowl over a pot of boiling water and continue to stir. This additional heat will help melt the remaining chocolate.
■ Melted milk chocolate may be too thick to coat the truffles. Add about a teaspoon of vegetable oil to thin it before dipping the chocolate balls.

Plan Ahead These will keep in the refrigerator for at least a week or two, if they aren't eaten first!

Variation Instead of coffee, use two tablespoons of dry red wine for a subtle fruity flavor in your truffles.

Chocolate
BARK

Pareve | **Yield** about 2 pounds

Bark is one of my favorite desserts to make. It looks elegant enough for sweet shops and chocolatiers to charge upwards of $10-15 per pound, but it's ridiculously easy to make — and it's so versatile! Here are four of my favorite ways to make bark, but you can have fun combining your favorite add-ins to come up with your own varieties.

melted chocolate for variation of your choice (see below and facing page)

toppings of your choice (see below and facing page)

1. Line a baking sheet with parchment paper.

2. Use a rubber or offset spatula to spread the chocolate in a thin layer over the parchment paper. It should cover most of the baking sheet.

3. Sprinkle toppings over chocolate, distributing them evenly. When making Salted White Chocolate Bark, swirl melted chocolate gently to lightly incorporate toppings.

4. Allow chocolate to set completely; break hardened bark into pieces.

SALTED WHITE CHOCOLATE BARK

2 cups good-quality white chocolate chips, melted

¾ cup Rice Krispies, crushed lightly by hand

1½-2 teaspoons coarse sea salt

S'MORES BARK

15 oz semisweet chocolate, melted

4 whole graham crackers, crushed into small pieces

1 cup mini marshmallows

For best results, reserve some melted chocolate to drizzle over the top of the S'mores Bark after it has hardened.

SWEET AND SALTY BARK

15 oz semisweet chocolate, melted

½ cup coarsely crushed pretzels

½ cup coarsely crushed potato chips

½ cup coarsely crushed popcorn

FRUIT AND NUT BARK

15 oz semisweet chocolate, melted

¾ cup raisins, dried cranberries, or chopped dried fruit of your choice

¾ cup mixed roasted, salted nuts

Notes ■ In addition to being a delicious candy all on its own, shards of bark make great decorations for cupcakes, layer cakes, mousse cups, and other desserts. ■ The toppings listed here are merely suggestions. Have fun mixing and matching the toppings of your choice, including cereal and candy.

Plan Ahead Bark keeps really well in an airtight container for about a week in the fridge, and even longer in the freezer.

Rice Krispie Treat
TRUFFLES

Dairy or **Pareve** | **Yield** 35-40 truffles

Rice Krispie Treats are an old favorite among kids and adults alike. In this great variation, that traditional favorite is elevated into an elegant and tasty party treat. As a bonus, the chocolate coating provides a nice textural contrast for the chewy treat on the inside. Here are two great flavor variations for one delicious treat.

CHOCOLATE RICE KRISPIE TREATS

4 cups crisp rice cereal

1½ cups marshmallow fluff

1 cup chocolate-hazelnut spread

1 Tablespoon oil

8 oz milk or semisweet chocolate, melted, for coating

PEANUT BUTTER RICE KRISPIE TREATS

4 cups crisp rice cereal

1½ cups marshmallow fluff

1 cup creamy peanut butter

1 Tablespoon oil

8 oz milk or semisweet chocolate, melted, for coating

1. Place cereal into a large bowl; set aside.

2. In a small pot over medium heat, melt together marshmallow fluff, chocolate-hazelnut spread OR peanut butter, and oil until smooth and fluff has melted. Immediately pour mixture over cereal; toss well to coat all cereal.

3. Working quickly before mixture sets completely, scoop it into small balls, about an inch to an inch and a half in diameter. This is easiest and most uniform when done with a medium cookie scoop. Set balls on parchment paper to set. Once all the balls have been formed, they should be firm enough to dip.

4. Dip each ball into melted chocolate, allowing the excess chocolate to drip off; then place the truffle on parchment paper until the chocolate hardens.

Note To make these truffles fancier, drizzle chocolate, white chocolate, or colored candy melts over the top.

Variation Instead of forming truffles, press the cereal mixture into a 9-inch square pan. Let set completely, then drizzle melted chocolate over the top. You won't need the full 8 ounces of chocolate for this variation.

Plan Ahead Truffles keep well in an airtight container in the refrigerator for a few days, and even longer in the freezer.

EASY HOMEMADE
Caramel Popcorn

Dairy or **Pareve** | **Yield** 8-9 cups

One of the great things about blogging is meeting amazing people, both in person, and online. One of the most extraordinary people I've encountered is Charles Sayegh, the teenage entrepreneur who sells delicious — and wildly popular — kosher frozen desserts under the name @FrozenExplosions. Starting at the age of 14, the now 11th-grade kid makes these pies between attending high school and studying. We connected over our mutual "overtime" status — working or studying full time, and running a food business after hours. He was kind enough to share this amazing caramel popcorn recipe.

POPCORN

3 Tablespoons oil

½ cup yellow popcorn kernels

CARAMEL

5 Tablespoons butter or trans-fat-free margarine

3 cups sugar

1 cup water

1½ Tablespoons kosher salt

½ teaspoon baking soda

1. Prepare the popcorn: Heat oil in a large pot over medium heat. To make sure oil is hot enough, drop in one corn kernel. When it pops, pour the rest of the kernels into the pot; cover pot.

2. Keeping the cover on, shake the pot to help popcorn pop evenly and prevent burning.

3. When the popping sound slows, remove pot from heat. Pour the popcorn into a large, greased, heatproof bowl.

4. Prepare the caramel: In a medium pot, melt butter over medium-high heat. Add sugar, water, and salt. Stir until sugar has dissolved.

5. Cook mixture over medium-high heat, **without stirring**, for 15-20 minutes, until it begins to brown around the edges.

6. Meanwhile, measure baking soda, grease two heatproof spatulas or spoons, and line a baking sheet with parchment paper. Coat parchment with nonstick cooking spray. Time is of the essence in the next step, so have everything handy and be ready to work quickly.

7. Once sugar mixture begins to brown around the edges, remove pot from heat; add baking soda. Whisk for about 10 seconds. Mixture will bubble vigorously and thicken. **Quickly** pour sugar mixture over popcorn and toss with the two prepared spatulas until all popcorn is evenly coated.

8. Pour popcorn onto prepared baking tray and set aside to cool. Once cooled, break into chunks and enjoy!

Note For easiest clean up, wash utensils immediately, before the sugar hardens.

Plan Ahead Store caramel popcorn in an airtight bag for up to a few days.

Chewy Sea Salt
CARAMELS

Dairy | **Yield** 40 caramels

Authentic chewy caramels are a special kind of indulgence. Their buttery flavor, combined with the dense, chewy texture, creates an amazing treat — and the sea salt really takes it over the top. They are sophisticated and pretty, and they make a great gift.

1 cup heavy cream

1 stick (½ cup) butter

1 cup brown sugar

½ cup sugar

½ cup light corn syrup

1 teaspoon vanilla extract

½ teaspoon coarse sea salt

SPECIAL EQUIPMENT

candy thermometer

1. Combine cream and butter in a medium pot over medium heat. Whisk until butter has melted. Pour mixture into a small bowl; set aside. No need to wash the pot before continuing with the recipe.

2. Place sugars and corn syrup into the same pot. Stir to combine. Cook over medium heat until mixture just starts to bubble. Add cream mixture; stir to combine.

3. Place candy thermometer into the pot. Wait for mixture to reach 255°F, 10-15 minutes. Keep a close watch! As the candy mixture heats, it will bubble vigorously. Do not stir the caramel during this time.

4. Meanwhile, line an 8-inch square pan with parchment paper, leaving some paper overhanging the sides. Grease the paper very well with nonstick cooking spray.

5. When the mixture reaches 255°F, immediately turn off the heat. Do not let the mixture become too hot, or your candy will be rock hard instead of chewy. (It's best to stay near the stove while candy is close to 255°F, so as not to risk overcooking it.)

6. Immediately stir vanilla into the candy mixture. Pour caramel into prepared pan. Place into the refrigerator to cool for about half an hour, then remove and sprinkle coarse salt over the top. Return to fridge to cool completely, for at least 2 hours or overnight.

7. Once the caramels have cooled, cut them into 1½-inches by ½-inch rectangles. Caramel is easiest to cut when very firm, so for best results, place in freezer for approximately a half hour before cutting.

Notes ■ Use a medium/large pot to prevent overflow, as the candy will bubble up while cooking. ■ To wrap: cut a square of wax paper about 3 inches wide. Place caramel on the edge and roll up paper. Twist sides to seal.

Variation Omit the sea salt for a more traditional caramel flavor.

Plan Ahead Store caramels in an airtight container in the refrigerator for up to 2 weeks.

Sweet and Spicy
ROASTED NUTS

Pareve | **Yield** 4 cups

All the desserts in this cookbook are pretty hard to resist, but there's something extra-tempting about these slightly sticky, slightly sweet, faintly spicy, and completely irresistible nuts. If you've never roasted nuts, try this easy recipe and you'll find out what you've been missing!

1 egg white

¼ cup pure maple syrup or honey

2 Tablespoons oil

2 Tablespoons brown sugar

2 teaspoons salt

1½ teaspoons cinnamon

½ teaspoon ground ginger

¼ teaspoon ground cayenne pepper

1 cup raw almonds

1 cup raw cashews

1 cup raw pecans

1 cup raw walnuts

1. Preheat oven to 350°F. Line a baking sheet with parchment paper; set aside.

2. In a medium bowl, whisk together egg white, maple syrup, oil, sugar, salt, and spices until smooth.

3. Add nuts; toss until all are evenly coated.

4. Spread nut mixture on prepared baking sheet. Bake for 8 minutes; then stir and bake for an additional 8 minutes. Nuts will be soft when they come out of the oven, but firm up as they cool.

5. Cool completely before serving.

Note The small amount of cayenne pepper imparts only a hint of heat, and it brings out the rest of the flavors in these nuts. However, if you really don't like the heat, reduce the amount to a pinch or omit cayenne altogether.

Variation You can switch the nut combinations and proportions depending on your preferences. Omit nuts you don't like, or use just one variety of your choosing.

Plan Ahead These nuts can be stored in an airtight container for up to one week.

■ Turn ice cream into an ice cream pie, using the method from the Pumpkin Ice Cream Pie (page 172) by softening ice cream in the flavor of your choice, until it's just soft enough to fill the crust. (Do not allow the ice cream to melt.) Transfer ice cream into a store-bought graham cracker crust; refreeze until firm. Cut into slices just before serving. You will need about 4 cups (1 quart) of ice cream to fill 1 graham cracker crust.

■ Feel free to switch up the drink recipes in this chapter. For example, use coffee ice cream in the Mocha Crunch Milkshake, or add additional fruits such as banana to the tropical fruit smoothies. Drink recipes are generally less of a science than baking recipes, so you can adapt these recipes as you like.

DRINKS *AND* FROZEN TREATS

- For the adults, feel free to add alcohol of your choice to the various drink recipes. Vodka and rum go well with the fruit drinks, while coffee and chocolate liqueur go well with the coffee drinks. Because you don't need to add the alcohol until the very end, you can easily share these drinks with children and add the alcohol to your own serving.

- If you're going to make homemade drinks fairly often, a good-quality blender is a worthwhile investment. (And at a savings of about five dollars per drink that you make instead of buy, it will pay for itself!) Look for a blender that comes with both single-serve cups and a larger size bowl, so you can make individual drinks or drinks for the whole family.

Pumpkin
ICE CREAM PIE

Dairy or **Pareve** | **Yield** 8-10 servings

Move over, traditional pumpkin pie! This ice cream variety needs no baking and is super simple to make. While homemade ice cream can be complicated to prepare and requires special equipment, this cool trick takes store-bought ice cream and makes it taste homemade. Because this pie has such amazing flavor, it's especially perfect for making with nondairy ice cream, which isn't that great on its own.

4 cups vanilla ice cream or nondairy ice cream

¾ cup canned pumpkin purée

¼ cup brown sugar

1½ teaspoons cinnamon

1 teaspoon ground ginger

½ teaspoon ground nutmeg

1 graham cracker pie crust

graham cracker crumbs, optional, for topping

1. Defrost ice cream until softened but not melted. Place into the bowl of a food processor fitted with the "S" blade.

2. Add pumpkin, sugar, cinnamon, ginger, and nutmeg. Process until mixture is smooth and all ingredients are combined.

3. Pour mixture into graham cracker crust. If desired, top with additional graham cracker crumbs. Freeze until ready to serve.

Note Be sure not to use canned pumpkin pie filling, as it has ingredients not needed here. Of course, homemade pumpkin purée is great, too.

Variation Freeze ice cream in a container instead of the pie crust; serve in cones or cups.

Plan Ahead Pie keeps well in the freezer. Slice just before serving.

Mocha
SORBET

Pareve | **Yield** 6-8 servings

This sorbet is so rich and creamy, you'll be amazed that it's "just" a sorbet, and not a heavy ice cream or chocolate mousse. Commercially bought chocolate or mocha sorbet isn't very tasty, but just try this one — you'll find the difference astonishing.

1½ cups sugar

⅔ cup cocoa powder

1 teaspoon vanilla extract

pinch salt

1 cup brewed coffee (or **1 Tablespoon** instant coffee granules dissolved in **1 cup** hot water)

1¼ cups boiling water

5 ounces semisweet chocolate, chopped

1 In a medium pot over medium heat, combine all ingredients except chocolate. Whisk until smooth.

2 Bring mixture to a boil, then immediately remove from heat. Quickly add chopped chocolate; stir until chocolate has melted and mixture is smooth.

3 If you have an ice cream maker, freeze the mixture according to machine directions; skip steps 4 and 5.

4 If you don't have an ice cream maker, line a baking sheet with foil. Spread the mixture on baking sheet and place in freezer for about 1 hour. After an hour, the mixture should be partially frozen. Remove from freezer and blend in food processor until smooth again.

5 Repeat the process of freezing and blending twice more, for a total of three times. After the third time blending, pour mixture into an airtight container; freeze until ready to serve.

Notes ■ The process of making sorbet without an ice cream machine might seem complicated, but it actually takes only a few minutes each time, so it's great to work on when you're around the house doing other things. ■ To save time washing dishes, don't bother washing the food processor between each step of blending.

Plan Ahead Store this sorbet in an airtight container in the freezer.

Mango Peach
SORBET

Pareve | **Yield** 6-8 servings

Mango Peach Sorbet is a light and refreshing dessert that really highlights the best of seasonal summer fruits, and it is easier to make than you may think!

2 cups mango, peeled and diced

2 cups peaches, peeled and diced

1 cup sugar

2 Tablespoons lemon or lime juice

1. Place mangoes and peaches into the bowl of a food processor fitted with the "S" blade. Purée for a minute or two, until mostly smooth.

2. Add sugar and lemon juice. Continue to purée until mixture is completely smooth. Depending on your food processor's capability, this can take a few minutes.

3. If you have an ice cream maker, freeze the mixture according to machine directions; skip steps 4 and 5.

4. If you don't have an ice cream maker, line a baking sheet with foil. Spread fruit mixture on baking sheet; place in freezer for about an hour. After an hour, the mixture should be partially frozen. Remove from freezer and blend in food processor until smooth.

5. Repeat the process of freezing and blending twice more, for a total of three times. After the third blending, pour mixture into an airtight container; freeze until ready to serve.

Note See Note on facing page.

Variation Use all mangoes or all peaches, if you prefer.

Plan ahead Store sorbet in an airtight container in the freezer.

Spiced 'n Spiked
HOT APPLE CIDER

Pareve | Yield 6-8 servings

This recipe started with hand cream. I know, it's a weird sentence, but here's the story. I was shopping with my friend Shaindy and purchased a bottle of Hot Apple Cider-scented hand cream. I put it on, and the smell was so incredible that Shaindy and I both started craving hot apple cider. The next day, we made this, and we've been making it ever since — it's the ultimate winter comfort drink!

½ **gallon** apple cider

2 oranges, sliced into rounds (peel on)

2 apples, sliced into rounds (peel on, core removed)

3-4 whole cinnamon sticks OR 2 teaspoons ground cinnamon

2-3 whole cloves OR ½ teaspoon ground cloves

½ teaspoon ground nutmeg

½ teaspoon ground ginger

rum, to taste, optional

1. In a large pot, combine apple cider, oranges, apples, and spices. Bring to a boil, then simmer for about half an hour.

2. Remove cinnamon sticks and whole cloves, if using. Pour cider into mugs. Add rum, if desired.

Plan Ahead
This is best made fresh, but if you have any left, bring it to a boil again before serving.

Orange
HOT CHOCOLATE

Dairy | Yield 4 servings

Hot chocolate conjures up the image of a cozy, lazy, snowy winter day. This version adds orange for an extra burst of flavor. If making this drink for kids, cook the mixture for an additional few minutes after adding the liquor to allow all alcohol to cook off.

4 cups milk

5 oz semisweet chocolate

1 cinnamon stick

scant ¼ cup orange liqueur (50 mL bottle)

zest of 1 orange, finely grated

1 In a small pot, combine milk, chocolate, and cinnamon. Bring to a boil; reduce heat to a simmer. Simmer over low heat, stirring occasionally, until chocolate has melted and mixture is fairly smooth.

2 Add liqueur and zest; cook for 5 minutes to integrate flavors.

3 Remove cinnamon stick and strain to remove zest. Serve hot.

Plan Ahead Store in the fridge. Bring to a boil just before serving.

177

Milkshakes

Dairy

A milkshake, at its simplest, is a combination of milk and ice cream that join together to make any meal more exciting. These milkshakes take it up a notch, with exciting flavors and textures.

Chocolate Peanut Butter
MILKSHAKE

Yield 2 servings

2 cups chocolate ice cream

2 Tablespoons creamy peanut butter

2 teaspoons chocolate syrup

½ cup milk

whipped cream and salted peanuts, chopped, to garnish (optional)

1. Add ingredients to a blender; blend until smooth.

2. Top with garnish, if desired.

Maple Bourbon
MILKSHAKE

Yield 2 servings

2 heaping Tablespoons candied pecans

2 cups vanilla ice cream

2 Tablespoons pure maple syrup

2 Tablespoons bourbon

¼ cup milk

whipped cream and candied pecans, chopped, to garnish (optional)

1. Add pecans to a blender; crush to form crumbs. Add remaining ingredients; blend until smooth.

2. Top with garnish, if desired.

Variation To lighten up these drinks, substitute sugar-free ice cream or frozen yogurt in any of the recipes. You can also save calories by omitting the garnishes and replacing the chocolate syrup with a sugar-free or reduced-calorie variety.

Strawberry Cheesecake
MILKSHAKE

Yield 2 servings

1 cup vanilla ice cream

6-8 frozen strawberries

2 Tablespoons cream cheese

½ cup milk

whipped cream and crushed graham crackers, to garnish (optional)

1   Add ingredients to a blender; blend until smooth.

2   Top with garnish, if desired.

Mocha Crunch *MILKSHAKE*

Yield 2 servings

4 chocolate sandwich cookies

¼ cup milk

2 cups chocolate ice cream

1 teaspoon instant coffee granules dissolved in ¼ cup boiling water

1 Tablespoon chocolate syrup

whipped cream and crushed sandwich cookies, to garnish (optional)

1   Add cookies to a blender; crush to form crumbs. Add remaining ingredients; blend until smooth.

2   Top with garnish, if desired.

Plan Ahead Milkshakes should be enjoyed freshly made.

Coffee DRINKS

If you've ever waited in a long line, then paid too much for your coffee, you'll want to try these variations instead. Whether you try the hot versions to warm you up on a cold day, or an iced drink to cool you down during the summer, these will please your palate and save your money.

Skinny Mocha *FRAPPE*

Dairy or **Pareve** | **Yield** 1 serving

2 Tablespoons unsweetened cocoa powder

2 teaspoons coffee granules

¼ cup boiling water

¼ cup sugar or other dry sweetener

1½ cups ice cubes

½ cup low-fat milk or soy milk

1. Combine cocoa, coffee, water, and sugar in a small bowl or cup. Stir to combine, breaking up as many lumps as possible.

2. Place ice, coffee mixture, and milk into a blender. Blend until combined.

3. Serve immediately.

Chocolate-Hazelnut *LATTE*

Dairy or **Pareve** | **Yield** 1 serving

1 shot espresso OR **2 teaspoons** instant coffee granules dissolved in **¼ cup** hot water

2 Tablespoons chocolate-hazelnut spread

¾ cup milk or soy milk

sugar, optional

1. Combine espresso and chocolate-hazelnut spread in a cup; stir until chocolate is dissolved and mixture is smooth.

2. Heat milk in microwave or with a foamer; add to coffee mixture. Sweeten to taste.

Note Take any of these drinks to the next level with a dollop of whipped cream, some Caramel or Chocolate Sauce (pages 194-195), or chocolate shavings.

Iced Vanilla *LATTE*

Dairy or **Pareve** | **Yield** 1 serving

1 Tablespoon instant coffee granules, preferably French Vanilla flavor

1 Tablespoon instant vanilla pudding mix (regular or sugar-free)

¼ cup boiling water

½ teaspoon vanilla extract

1 heaping cup ice cubes

½ cup milk, skim milk, or soy milk

whipped cream, for serving, optional

1. In a small cup, combine coffee, pudding mix, and water. Stir until smooth; it should gel and be fairly smooth. (Don't worry if there are a couple of lumps, though; they'll break up when you blend them.)

2. Place the coffee mixture, vanilla, ice, and milk into a blender. Blend until smooth and creamy.

3. Pour into a cup; top with whipped cream, if using. Serve immediately.

White Chocolate Peppermint *LATTE*

Dairy | **Yield** 2 servings

4 teaspoons instant coffee granules dissolved in ½ cup hot water

¼ cup chopped white chocolate or white chocolate chips

1½ cups milk

½ teaspoon mint extract

¼ teaspoon vanilla extract (optional)

whipped cream, optional, for garnish

crushed peppermint candies, optional, for garnish

1. In a small pot, combine coffee, white chocolate, and milk. Stir over medium heat until white chocolate has melted and mixture is smooth.

2. Add mint and vanilla extracts; top with whipped cream and crushed candies, if using. Serve hot.

Plan Ahead For maximum enjoyment, all the coffee drinks on these pages are best when made fresh.

Fruit *DRINKS*

Pareve

These drinks are bursting with flavor, look beautiful, and really turn an ordinary meal into a special occasion. Add a slice of fruit to the rim of the glass for an elegant presentation.

Tropical Fruit *SMOOTHIE*

Yield 2-3 servings

½ cup frozen strawberries

½ cup frozen mango chunks

½ cup frozen peach slices

½ cup frozen or canned pineapple chunks

1¼ cups orange juice

1 Place all ingredients into a blender.

2 Blend until completely smooth.

Cherry Limeade *SLUSHIES*

Yield 1-2 servings

1 cup frozen cherries

2 Tablespoons lime juice

½ cup ice cubes

1 cup water

2 Tablespoons sugar or sweetener

1 Place all ingredients into a blender. Blend until smooth.

2 Serve immediately.

Variation Adults can enhance any of these drinks with the addition of an alcoholic beverage such as vodka or rum.

Peach *ICED TEA*

Yield 6 servings

1 ripe peach, peeled, halved, and pitted

½ cup boiling water

8 bags black tea

6 cups boiling water

⅓ cup sugar or other dry sweetener

1 teaspoon lemon juice

ice cubes, optional, for serving

1. Place peach and water into a blender; purée until smooth. Set aside.

2. Place tea bags into a large pitcher; pour boiling water over tea bags. Brew at room temperature for 30 minutes. Add reserved peach purée, sugar and lemon juice, stirring to combine. Refrigerate until chilled.

3. Serve over ice, if desired.

Watermelon *LEMONADE*

Yield 10 servings

4 cups watermelon, cut into 1-inch cubes

1 cup sugar

1 cup water

1 cup lemon juice

7-9 cups water, to taste

1. Place watermelon cubes into the bowl of a food processor fitted with the "S" blade. Purée until smooth. Strain to remove all solids. About 2 cups liquid should remain. Set aside.

2. In a small pot, combine sugar and water. Stir occasionally over medium heat until mixture comes to a boil and sugar has dissolved. Let cool for five minutes; add lemon juice.

3. Place watermelon juice and lemon mixture into a large pitcher. Add 7-9 cups water, depending on how strongly flavored you like it. Stir to combine.

4. Chill. Serve over ice.

Plan Ahead Cherry Limeade Slushies and Tropical Fruit Smoothies should be enjoyed fresh. Peach Iced Tea and Watermelon Lemonade can be stored in the fridge for up to a week.

- While the recipes on the following pages don't stand alone, they will transform the treats in the preceding sections into beautiful and completed edible creations. Look throughout the book for suggested toppings to try with the recipes, or mix and match these frostings and glazes with your existing family favorite cakes and desserts.

- Homemade sauces (pages 194-195) are immeasurably better than those you will buy from the store, so when you're making a dessert that really needs to impress, make a batch of sauce to complement it.

- Frosted cakes and cupcakes don't store or travel very well, so I like to store and travel with them unfrosted. Prepare the frosting ahead of time, and keep it in an airtight container in the fridge. Bring it with you, along with a piping bag, and take a couple of minutes to pipe them just before serving. They'll look better, and you won't have to stress about your hard work being ruined.

FROSTINGS *AND* TOPPINGS

Royal
ICING

Pareve | **Yield** icing to decorate one batch of No-Margarine Sugar Cookies

There's a good reason that royal icing cookies are a perennial favorite at parties and dessert tables. First, they're endlessly versatile: using any shaped cookie, combined with any combination of colors and designs, you can match any occasion or theme. The other great thing about royal icing is that it dries completely hard, so the cookies can be packed up easily, and stay fresh for a week or more.

4 cups powdered sugar

2 Tablespoons meringue powder (see Note)

6 Tablespoons water

½ teaspoon clear flavor extract, optional

food coloring, preferably gel, optional

No-Margarine Sugar Cookies (page 42), to decorate

SPECIAL EQUIPMENT, OPTIONAL

piping bags

thin piping tips

squeeze bottles

toothpicks

1 | In the bowl of a mixer, combine sugar, meringue powder, water and flavoring. Beat on medium-high speed for about 8 minutes, until the mixture no longer looks glossy. Test if the icing is ready: when you lift the beaters, the icing should hold its shape and form a peak that does not fall back at all.

2 | If using multiple colors, divide the icing into bowls, one for each color you will use. Add a few drops of food coloring to each bowl; mix until color is evenly distributed. To prevent hardening, tightly cover bowls when not in use.

3 | [A] Set baked cookies on a clear work surface with your tools and icings handy.

4 | Outlining: [B] Place a small amount of icing into a piping bag fitted with a very fine tip. A #3 tip is best for outlining. Hold the piping bag about a half an inch from the cookie; draw a line of icing around the edge of the cookie, forming a thin outline of the shape. Repeat with remaining cookies.

Notes ▪ More than most desserts, this recipe is a craft and an art form, and you'll get better with practice. Don't be discouraged if your first few cookies — or even batches — aren't perfect; even master cookie decorators started with imperfect cookies. ▪ When allowing cookies to dry overnight between steps, store unused icing in the fridge. Once thinned to flooding consistency, icing should be used that day. ▪ Meringue powder is a specialty egg-based baking product used in place of raw egg whites. It can be purchased in specialty kitchen stores or craft stores.

Plan Ahead Royal icing decorations maintain their shape and color for weeks, but for freshness, store them for about a week at room temperature. Iced cookies can be frozen, but some colors may leak slightly during the freezing process.

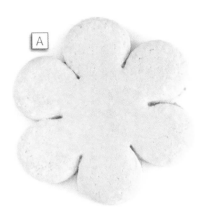

Flooding: [C] Use the same color of icing as the outline for flooding. Add a few drops of water to thin the icing until it is a thick liquid consistency. Test texture by drizzling some icing back into the bowl. It should disappear into the icing in about ten seconds. Place icing into a squeeze bottle and squeeze it out within the outline, "flooding" most of the cookie with icing. Use a toothpick to guide icing toward any empty spots and to meet the edges and corners of the outline. Let this layer harden completely, preferably overnight, before continuing. Do not touch the icing during this time; if you do, it may not dry smoothly.

Decorating: Once the base of the icing has completely hardened, you can add decorations. The process for this is similar to the outlining process. Use a very thin tip (a #1 or #2 tip is best for decorations, depending on how thin and intricate you want them to be). Draw a pattern [D] onto the cookie, in the shape and color of your choice. If desired, add additional accents [E] but allow each layer or decoration to dry before adding the next. If adding sugar pearls, sanding sugar, or other decorations [F], add while the icing is still wet, as the icing will act as the glue for the decorations.

Once decorations are complete, let the cookies air dry for at least a few hours, preferably overnight, to ensure that the icing is completely hard before you wrap them.

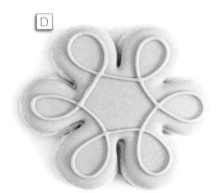

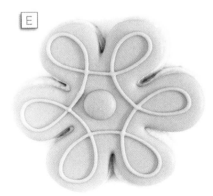

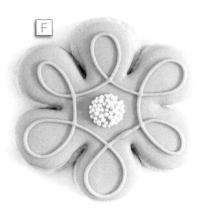

Frostings

Dairy or **Pareve**

Mix and match the flavors of these frostings with your favorite cakes, cookies, and cupcakes from Chapters One and Two. To create a flavor that isn't here, use the Marshmallow Fluff Frosting recipe and add your choice of flavor extracts. Because they're white, both the Marshmallow Fluff Frosting and the Cream Cheese Frosting lend themselves well to coloring, if you'd like to match your party colors or decor.

Chocolate Fudge
FROSTING

Yield 2 cups

2 sticks (1 cup) butter or trans-fat-free margarine

½ cup cocoa powder

1 teaspoon vanilla extract

½ teaspoon salt

2½ cups powdered sugar

1. In the bowl of an electric mixer fitted with the whisk attachment, on high speed, beat together butter, cocoa, vanilla, and salt until combined.

2. Reduce mixer speed. Gradually add powdered sugar; beat until fluffy.

Marshmallow Fluff
FROSTING

Yield 2 cups

2 sticks (1 cup) butter or trans-fat-free margarine

1 cup marshmallow fluff

1 teaspoon vanilla extract

½ teaspoon flavor extract, optional

food coloring, optional

2 cups powdered sugar

1. In the bowl of an electric mixer fitted with the whisk attachment, on high speed, beat together butter, marshmallow fluff, and vanilla until combined. Add flavor extract and food coloring, if using.

2. Reduce mixer speed. Gradually add powdered sugar; beat until fluffy.

Chocolate Fudge Frosting

Peanut Butter Frosting *p. 32*

Marshmallow Fluff Frosting

Salted Caramel
FROSTING

Yield 3 cups

3 sticks (1½ cups) butter or trans-fat-free margarine, divided

¾ cup brown sugar

2 Tablespoons milk or soy milk

1½ teaspoons kosher salt

1 teaspoon vanilla extract

3 cups powdered sugar

1. In a small pot, over medium heat, melt together 1 stick butter and sugar until melted and combined (fat may separate). Add milk; continue to cook for a few minutes until mixture is thick and bubbling. Remove from heat; set aside to cool for about half an hour.

2. In the bowl of an electric mixer fitted with the whisk attachment, on high speed, beat together remaining 2 sticks butter, salt, and vanilla until smooth. With the mixer running, slowly pour in the caramel mixture; beat until smooth.

3. Reduce mixer speed. Gradually add powdered sugar; beat until fluffy.

Cream Cheese
FROSTING

Yield 3 cups

2 sticks (1 cup) butter or trans-fat-free margarine

8 ounces cream cheese or soy cream cheese

1 teaspoon vanilla extract

½ teaspoon salt

2½ cups powdered sugar

1. In the bowl of an electric mixer fitted with the whisk attachment, on high speed, beat together butter, cream cheese, vanilla, and salt until combined.

2. Reduce mixer speed. Gradually add powdered sugar; beat until fluffy.

Plan Ahead Store frostings in an airtight container in the fridge for up to a week. For best results, frost baked goods within a day or two of serving.

Salted Caramel Frosting

Strawberry Frosting *p. 86*

Cream Cheese Frosting

Glazes

Dairy or **Pareve** | **Yield** Each glaze yields enough to glaze 1 standard cake

Glazes are formed when the correct proportions of powdered sugar and liquid are combined. I've provided a number of flavor options to get you started, but feel free to play around with your favorite flavors. If you feel that your glaze is too thin to hold up well or too thick to drizzle, add a little more powdered sugar or liquid, respectively, to attain the perfect texture.

Vanilla GLAZE

1 cup powdered sugar

1 Tablespoon light corn syrup or honey

1 Tablespoon milk or soy milk

½ teaspoon vanilla extract

1 Combine all ingredients in a small bowl.

2 Whisk until smooth.

Brown Sugar GLAZE

2 Tablespoons butter or trans-fat-free margarine

½ cup brown sugar

1 teaspoon vanilla extract

1 cup powdered sugar

1½ Tablespoons milk or soy milk

1 In a small pot, over medium heat, melt together margarine and brown sugar until smooth. Remove from heat; add vanilla. Set aside to cool for a couple of minutes.

2 Combine brown sugar mixture, powdered sugar, and milk in a small bowl.

3 Whisk until smooth.

Cream Cheese *GLAZE*

2 ounces cream cheese or soy cream cheese	**1** Combine all ingredients in a small bowl.
1¼ cups powdered sugar	
½ teaspoon vanilla extract	**2** Whisk until smooth.
1 Tablespoon milk or soy milk	

Chocolate *GLAZE*

1 cup powdered sugar	**1** Combine all ingredients in a small bowl.
2 Tablespoons unsweetened cocoa powder	
2 Tablespoons milk or soy milk	**2** Whisk until smooth.

Coffee *GLAZE*

1 cup powdered sugar	**1** Combine all ingredients in a small bowl.
1 teaspoon instant coffee granules dissolved in 4 teaspoons hot water	
1 Tablespoon oil	**2** Whisk until smooth.
½ teaspoon vanilla extract	

Cinnamon Spice *GLAZE*

1 cup powdered sugar

1 Tablespoon molasses

1 teaspoon cinnamon

2 teaspoons milk or soy milk

½ teaspoon ground ginger

½ teaspoon ground nutmeg

a pinch ground cloves

1. Combine all ingredients in a small bowl.

2. Whisk until smooth.

Peanut Butter *GLAZE*

1 cup powdered sugar

2 Tablespoons creamy peanut butter

2 Tablespoons warm water

½ teaspoon vanilla extract

1. Combine all ingredients in a small bowl.

2. Whisk until smooth.

Maple *GLAZE*

1 cup powdered sugar

1 Tablespoon pure maple syrup

½ teaspoon cinnamon

2 teaspoons milk or soy milk

½ teaspoon ground ginger

1. Combine all ingredients in a small bowl.

2. Whisk until smooth.

Note As you make your glaze, gradually add additional liquid or sugar, if needed, to achieve the perfect texture. I like my glazes on the thick side, so they hold their shape well.

Honey *GLAZE*

1 cup powdered sugar	**1** Combine all ingredients in a small bowl.
1 Tablespoon honey	
1 teaspoon cinnamon	
2 teaspoons milk or soy milk	**2** Whisk until smooth.

Citrus *GLAZE*

1 cup powdered sugar	**1** Combine all ingredients in a small bowl.
1 teaspoon citrus juice, such as lemon, lime, or orange	
2 teaspoons finely grated citrus zest	**2** Whisk until smooth.
1 Tablespoon light corn syrup or honey	
1 Tablespoon hot water	

Customizable *GLAZE*

1 cup powdered sugar	**1** Combine all ingredients in a small bowl.
1 Tablespoon light corn syrup or honey	
1 Tablespoon milk or soy milk	**2** Whisk until smooth.
½ teaspoon clear flavor extract of your choice	
2-3 drops food coloring, optional	

Plan Ahead Store glazes in an airtight container in fridge for up to a week. If the glaze thickens, add a few drops of liquid to bring it back to the right consistency.

Sauces

Dairy or **Pareve**

A great way to transform a dessert from "great" to "absolutely amazing" is to use homemade sauces. Drizzle these sauces over your dessert, use them to decorate the plates, or even pour on as a phenomenal ice cream topper.

Caramel *SAUCE*

Yield about 1 cup

1 cup brown sugar

½ stick (¼ cup) butter or trans-fat-free margarine

¼ cup heavy cream or nondairy whip topping

1. In a small pot, over medium heat, combine the brown sugar and butter. Stir until butter has melted. When the mixture starts to bubble slightly around the edges, add cream; whisk until combined. Simmer for an addional 2-3 minutes, until thickened.

2. Serve immediately or store in fridge until ready to serve

Note Caramel sauce will harden in the fridge, so bring it back to room temperature or reheat in a microwave or over a low flame before using.

Plan Ahead Store all of these sauces in an airtight container in the fridge for up to a week.

Strawberry *SAUCE*

Yield about 2 cups

1 lb fresh or frozen
strawberries
(defrosted),
finely chopped

½ cup sugar

2 Tablespoons
lemon juice

finely grated zest of
½ orange, optional

1 Place all ingredients
into a saucepan; stir
well until combined.

2 Simmer over low
to medium heat for
about 20 minutes,
until the liquid
emitted by the
berries has been
partially reabsorbed
and the sauce
becomes thicker.

3 If you prefer a
smooth sauce,
blend it in the
blender or food
processor.

Chocolate *SAUCE*

Yield about 2½ cups

¾ cup unsweetened
cocoa powder

1¾ cup sugar

1⅓ cups milk
or soy milk

1½ teaspoons
vanilla extract

1 In a medium pot,
over medium heat,
combine cocoa,
sugar, and milk.
Whisk until smooth.
Bring to a boil; reduce
heat to a simmer.
Simmer for 5-6
minutes, stirring
occasionally, until
mixture is thick and
bubbling.

2 Remove from heat
and stir in vanilla. Use
hot or store in fridge
until ready to use.

Holiday Guide

Planning, cooking, and baking your holiday meals can feel overwhelming, so here's a guide to help make it all a little easier. When planning ahead for holiday cooking, I always like to prepare the desserts and baked goods first and get them out of the way, as many desserts can easily be frozen. Use the **Plan Ahead** tips on each page to help you determine which treats to make and freeze ahead of time.

ROSH HASHANAH

Rosh Hashanah is a great time to enjoy fall flavors, as the summer ends and the weather starts to change. In addition, there are a number of traditional foods to enjoy on Rosh Hashanah, including apples, honey, and pomegranates. Here are some of my favorites.

Chocolate Chunk Honey Cookies (page 28)

Apple Pie Thumbprint Cookies (page 38)

Caramel Apple Bundt Cake (page 60)

Honey Sour Cream Bundt Cake (page 68)

Pomegranate Cupcakes (page 84)

Braided Apple Pie (page 120)

p. 120

p. 84

p. 28

p. 60

SUCCOS

Succos can be tricky to prepare desserts for, as it's between seasons. Sometimes you'll want a cool, refreshing dessert, and other times, you'll want to serve a warm, comforting dessert. Plan to have a selection of each, and serve them based on the mealtime temperature. Try these weather-appropriate favorites.

WARM DESSERTS

Cinnamon Cheese Buns
(page 98)

Hot Gooey Caramel Pie
(page 110)

Cookie Dough Fudge Pie
(page 112)

Pecan Pie Cigars
(page 154)

COLD/REFRESHING DESSERTS

Mini Fruit-Filled Pavlovas
(page 115)

Neapolitan Trifles (page 120)

Egg-Free Chocolate Mousse
(page 130)

Lemon Cheesecake Mousse Cups
(page 132)

Pumpkin Ice Cream Pie (page 172)

p. 98   p. 154   p. 120
p. 110
p. 172   p. 130
p. 132

TU B'SHVAT

This holiday celebrates fruit trees — specifically, those of the land of Israel. Here are some appropriate options to serve on Tu B'Shvat.

Pomegranate Cupcakes
(page 84)

Fruit pies (pages 116-122)

Chocolate Crepes
filled with fruit of your choice
(page 148)

Mini Fruit-Filled Pavlovas
(page 150)

Fruit and Nut Bark (page 160)

p. 150
p. 118
p. 116
p. 148

CHANUKAH

Food for Chanukah is all about the oil! Chanukah is also a time for parties, so it's a great time to test your decorating skills.

Chanukah Gelt Thumbprint Cookies: Bake **Apple Thumbprint Cookies** (page 38) without filling. As soon as they come out of the oven, press a small chocolate coin into the indentation of each cookie. The heat of the cookie will melt the chocolate slightly, causing it to adhere to the cookie.

Lemon Olive Oil Biscotti (page 41)

Royal Icing Cookies: (use **No-Margarine Sugar Cookies** on page 42, **Royal Icing** instructions on page 186) You can use Chanukah-shaped cookie cutters (such as a menorah or a dreidel) to make Chanukah cookies. Another fun idea is to make "donut cookies" by cutting circles of dough and then cutting smaller circles out of the centers. Instead of royal icing, decorate using **glazes** (pages 190-193) and your choice of sprinkles.

Bakery Style Cake Donuts (page 104)

p. 104

PURIM

Purim is a time of giving food gifts to family and friends — and sweets make great gifts. Most of the items in the book make great *mishloach manos* gifts, specifically, anything from the Candy and Chocolate section starting on page 156. Here are some additional suggestions for delicious — and show-stopping — *mishloach manos*.

Mini bundt cakes (pages 54-68) are a great *mishloach manos* item. They generally need a little less than half of the baking time of a full-size bundt cake.

Try one of these alcohol-infused treats for your *mishloach manos* or Purim party:

Bourbon Pecan Snowball Cookies (page 36)

Brown Sugar Rum Bundt Cake (page 58)

Hamantashen: Use the dough from the **Chocolate Cheesecake Pinwheel Cookies** (page 144). Cut out circles and place a small amount of filling in the center. Pinch the sides together to form the hamantasch shape. Bake for 10-12 minutes.

Red Wine Chocolate Truffles (page 158, see Variation)

p. 58

p. 36

p. 158

PASSOVER

Passover desserts can be challenging due to the restrictions on using flour and other ingredients. While this isn't specifically a Passover cookbook, there are a number of recipes that you can enjoy during this holiday.

Flourless Fudge Cookies (page 26) Ashkenazic Jews should use cashew butter or almond butter

Egg-Free Chocolate Mousse (page 130)

Mini Fruit-Filled Pavlovas (page 150) Use potato starch instead of corn starch.

Chocolate Truffles (page 158) or **Red Wine Truffles** (see Variation)

Fruit and Nut Bark (page 160)

Sweet and Salty Bark (page 160) (omit pretzels and popcorn; use only potato chips in the topping). For a great sweet and salty treat, you can also dip potato chips in chocolate and allow them to set.

Sweet and Spicy Roasted Nuts (page 168) Substitute honey if you can't find or don't use maple syrup.

Mocha Sorbet (page 174)

Mango Peach Sorbet (page 175)

Many of the **Drinks** on pages 176-183 can be made on Passover.

p. 26

p. 168

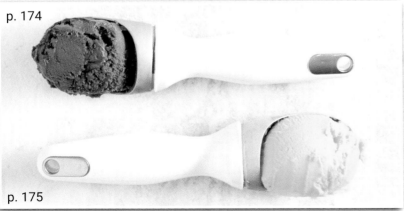

p. 174

p. 175

p. 160

p. 160

SHAVUOS

Dairy cooking is a big theme on Shavuos, and it's a great time to indulge in recipes that you might not eat on a daily basis. Most recipes that can be made pareve are even more delicious when made dairy, so take your pick! Some of my favorites include:

Chocolate Cheesecake Pinwheel Cookies (page 44)

Cinnamon Cheese Buns (page 98)

Cream Cheese Rugelach (page 100)

No-Fail Flaky Pie Crust (page 114) Homemade buttery pie crust is an incredible treat! Enjoy it baked with your choice of fillings (pages 116-122).

Praline Cannoli (page 134)

Pretzel Crusted Peanut Butter Cheesecake (page 140)

Neapolitan Zebra Cheesecake (page 142)

Chocolate Truffles (page 158)

Chewy Sea Salt Caramels (page 166) These are made only dairy, and they are an incredible and holiday-worthy indulgence.

p. 44

p. 134

p. 142

p. 100

p. 166

PLATED DESSERTS

If you're looking to end a meal in an impressive manner, whether at a party such as a *sheva brachos*, or a beautiful holiday meal, here are some great options. See page 126 for plating tips.

Chocolate Chip Peanut Pie (page 108) Serve with a dollop of whipped cream and some chopped salted or candied peanuts.

Hot Gooey Caramel Pie (page 110) Serve with a scoop of ice cream and a drizzle of caramel syrup or chocolate syrup. For a prettier presentation, bake the pies in mini graham cracker shells or ramekins (see Variation).

Cookie Dough Fudge Pie (page 112) Serve with a dollop of whipped cream or a scoop of ice cream. Drizzle with chocolate or caramel syrup.

Fruit pies (pages 116-122) Serve a slice of pie, warm, with whipped cream or ice cream on the side.

Salted Chocolate Peanut Butter Tartlets (page 124) Serve these whole or cut in half, topped with whipped cream or ice cream.

Neapolitan Trifles (page 128) These are beautiful and impressive as a dessert. Serve them in a mason jar for a more casual look, or use an elegant jar or stemmed glass for a more sophisticated party.

Lemon Cheesecake Mousse Cups (page 132) Create individual trifles by layering the mousse with crumbled Triple Citrus Bundt Cake (page 66) in a jar or glass.

Edible Cookie Cups (page 138) Fill the cups with ice cream, your choice of **Mousse** (pages 128-136), or **Mocha Sorbet** (page 174). Drizzle with **Caramel**, **Chocolate**, or **Strawberry Sauce** (pages 194-195) to match the flavor of the filling.

Chocolate Crepes (page 148) Serve filled and folded, with your choice of fillings and toppings.

Mini Fruit-Filled Pavlovas (page 150) These are great as shown as a light finish to a heavy meal. You can dress up the plate with **Strawberry Sauce** (page 195).

Pecan Pie Cigars (page 154)

p. 112

p. 124

p. 138

Party Guide
SETTING UP A
BEAUTIFUL DESSERT TABLE
PRO-TIPS FROM PARTY-PLANNER CHAVI CHASE

COLOR

- A color scheme of 2-3 colors enhances your display and helps pull all the elements together.

- When choosing your color scheme, take into account both the current season and the occasion.

- Printed tablecloths can be very eye-catching and pretty, but make sure they don't detract from the main attraction — the desserts!

- A runner in a color that complements the tablecloth goes a long way toward creating visual interest on your display.

- For tips on creating treats that match your color scheme, see facing page.

DESIGN

- When setting up the dessert table, think about what your focal point should be, and be sure to place your most beautiful desserts there.

- Keep accessibility in mind when placing your desserts. Even if the arrangement will look pretty, beware of placing edibles in a location that will be hard for your guests to reach.

- Use simple dishes in black, white, glass, or lucite, so as not to take the focus off the desserts.

- For a sleek, modern, and uniform look, group similar items together.

- Treats such as ***cupcakes*** (pages 82-86), ***pavlovas*** (page 150), and ***mini cakes*** (page 198; see Variation) should be placed in neat rows on flat surfaces or trays.

- Items such as **cookies** (pages 16-44) and **truffles** (pages 158, 162) can be piled on a tray or placed in a glass jar or container.

- Desserts in jars such as **Neapolitan Trifles** (page 128), **mousse cups** (pages 130-136), and fancy **drinks** (pages 176-183) can be placed directly on the table. Line them up in neat rows for maximum visual appeal. If you have different flavors of a similar item (such as mousse cups) alternate rows of different flavors.

- Create drama through height. Use containers of varying shapes and heights, and add tall elements, such as a vase of flowers, for additional height.

FOOD

COLOR-COORDINATED PARTY TREATS

- Make sandwich cookies using **Chocolate Chip Cookies** (page 20) or **Chocolate Chunk Chocolate Cookies** (page 22) and **Marshmallow Fluff Frosting** (page 188). Use food coloring to tint the frosting to match your party.

- Coat **Chocolate Truffles** (page 158) or **Rice Krispie Treat Truffles** (page 162) in milk or dark chocolate; then drizzle cooled truffles with colored candy melts to match your color scheme.

- Mini cupcakes make a great party treat. Bake mini **Chocolate Cupcakes** (page 86) or mini **Vanilla Cupcakes** (page 65); then top them with tinted **Marshmallow Fluff Frosting** (page 188). If making Vanilla Cupcakes, you can use a couple of drops of food coloring in the batter to tint the cake as well.

- Use the **Royal Icing Guide** (page 186) to create cookies that match the color and theme of your event.

INDIVIDUAL PARTY TREATS

- **Mousse** (pages 128-136) served in a small (approximately 2-ounce) glass is a great party treat.

- **Hand pies** (page 118; also see Variations) are delicious and look beautiful at parties.

- Elegant cookies such as **Chocolate Cheesecake Pinwheel Cookies** (page 44), **Tiramisu Cookies** (page 34), **Bourbon Pecan Snowball Cookies** (page 36), and **Apple Pie Thumbprint Cookies** (page 38) are great for a dessert table.

- Serve **Watermelon Lemonade** (page 183) or **Peach Iced Tea** (page 183) in small glass bottles or a glass beverage dispenser.

Index

Note: Page references in **bold** refer to recipe variations.

Thank you to my recipe testers for generously giving their time to bake and evaluate the recipes in this book. Your comments and suggestions have enhanced this book and ensure that every recipe will be enjoyed to its fullest.

Adina Zoltan Shyovitz, Ahuva Gottdiener, Aimee Baron, Alexis Baron, Aliza Schwartz, Amy Jacobs, Andrea Brown, Batsheva Katz, Bina Ilowitz, Bina Oscherowitz, Brani Bleiberg, Bryna Webb, Chana Gorin, Chani Eisenbach, Chavy Rottenberg, Chaya Braver, Cheved Greenwald, Daffy Yahalom, Danit Bermish, Devora Strauss, Devorah Muller, Devorie Newman, Donna Karp, Dvora Friedman, Elisa Gurevich, Ellen Zipkin, Esther Kleinman, Esther Simon, Esty Fried, Esty Leonerowitz, Faigy Murray, Faygie Friedman, Frumie Goodman, Henna Shomer, Henny Goldberger, Ida Eleff, Ilana Talitian, Karen Abishira, Karen Reiner, Lea Sod, Leah Epstein, Libby Weiss, Lisa Strimber, Maggie Gertel, Malki Fisher, Marnie Levy, Marsha Johnston, Meechal Roizman, Michal Hassan, Miriam Hecht, Miriam Malool, Miriam Rosenthal, Miriam Weg, Moshe Statman, Natalie Hirschel, Patricia Kadoche, Perela Dunoff, Rachel Seliger, Rivky Raichik, Roberta Schwartz, Rochel Leah Neuman, Rochie Krinsky, Ruchie Szlafrok, Ruthy Bodner, Samantha Gerstle, Sara Jacobs, Sarah Mizrahi, Sarah Nussbaum, Sarah Wieder, Shaina Gordon, Shaindel Lieberman, Shaindy Niederman, Shaindy Siegal, Shana Stavsky, Shani Rumstein, Shayna Margo, Shayndy Abrahamson, Shoshana Gifter, Shoshana Sturm, Susie Baumohl, Toby Wieder, Tova Friedman, Tova Fruchter, Tova Kwiat, Tzippi Robinson, Tzipporah Kranz, Yael Bendahan, Yael Ellis, Yael Neiman, Yael Zoldan, Yedida Orlofsky, Yehudis Bernhaut, Yehudis Stern, Yona Sternstein, Zehava Pasternak

Thank you to Miriam Rosenthal for coordinating everything!